A HOUSE IN THE SUNFLOWERS

A House in the Sunflowers

An English family's search for their
dream house in France

RUTH SILVESTRE

Illustrated by Michael Grater

ALLISON & BUSBY

An Allison & Busby book
Published in 1991 by
Virgin Publishing Ltd
26 Grand Union Centre
338 Ladbroke Grove
London W10 5AH

Reprinted 1991

Copyright © 1990 by Ruth Silvestre
Illustrations copyright © 1990 by Michael Grater

Typeset by Avocet Robinson, Buckingham
Printed in Great Britain by Mackays of Chatham PLC,
Chatham, Kent

ISBN 0 74900 088 0 PB

1

*S*ummer is over. It is late October and once again we are packing up the house. We are making our preparations to return to London, to spend the winter in 'the smoke' and, as always, wondering why. We are reluctant to acknowledge that as the days shorten and the temperature drops, and life must be lived indoors, we will need those other stimuli which only the city can provide. Yet, looking up at the wide blue sweep of sky where a pair of finches trill ecstatically on the wire, we dread the change, wonder how long it will take us to adjust this time and what it would be like simply to stay on.

We have spent the last twelve summers in our second home in this wonderfully unspoiled region of south west France where history seems to stalk the narrow village streets. I feel it when I am shopping in Monflanquin as I walk under the shadowed archway of the Black Prince's house, or in the sudden view of the great castle of Bonaguil, built high on a rock in a lush, wooded valley by one Berenger de Roquefeuil, last impassioned defender of an already outdated feudal system; or, yet again, when I see the eloquent line of upstretched arms on the memorial in the village of La Capelle Biron from where, one Sunday in May 1944, all the men were deported.

This year it will be even harder to return to England for we have been here now for three months, our longest stay so far. Our neighbouring farmer friends, who over the years have become like family, have complained each year. 'You always leave too early. Why don't you stay for *la vendange*? It's the best harvest of them all.'

With them we have shared the gathering in of almost everything that grows in this region of *la polyculture*. We've helped with the hay, the straw, tobacco, potatoes, the massive plum crop and the maize. We have watched the sunflowers turn from golden splendour to a desiccated umber before they fall beneath the combine and leave the fields silver with tough dry quills like a porcupine.

There are so many machines now. Many more than there were twelve years ago. Machines to cut and separate and spit out what is valuable into containers, leaving the residue for yet another machine to chop and chew and return to the soil. Raymond, our farmer, is proud of them. Some he owns, others he shares with a small group of neighbouring farms.

'So – what's so special about *la vendange*?' we ask again. 'Another new machine?'

'No, no.' He and his wife Claudette shrug and laugh, almost embarrassed. They cannot explain. And so we stayed to find the answer.

Last week, my arms covered in copper sulphate, I harvested grapes from early morning until I watched the last load tumble from the trailer into the screw of the giant mincer at the local *Cave Coopérative des Sept Monts*. The red sun slithered down behind the hill-top town of Monflanquin and darkness crept like a moth's wing across the fields. Monflanquin, Montagnac, Monsegur, Monreal, Monsempron, Montayral, Monbaillou – the litany of names of *les Sept Monts* after which the *Cave Coopérative* is named;

6

each a small ancient town, built on a gentle undulation rather than a steep hill, in this lovely corner of France between the rivers Lot and Garonne.

The vineyard, which had once been part of our property, is in a magnificent situation high on a south-facing slope. On a clear day you can see the Chateau of Biron on the horizon. The air was sweet and clean and, walking down to join the others, secateurs in pocket and basket in hand on a calm October morning, the sun dispersing the last traces of mist, I wondered why I ever wanted to be anywhere else.

For the *vendange* we were a group of about twenty, most of whom I recognised; Raymond and Claudette, the patron and his wife, and Lucienne his mother-in-law, frail and bent in her wellingtons and battered straw hat with its jaunty band of flowered cotton. There was small but stalwart Fernande from the next village with her wide, leathery face and wrinkled stockings and, dwarfing her completely, Mme Barrou who farms just outside our village and is famous for her conversation and her carrots. Huge, broad-shouldered and affectionate, she wrapped me in her strong arms and kissed me warmly.

'*Ça va? Et alors vous allez vendanger?*'

'*Ça va. Oui. C'est la première fois.* It's the first time I've done this. You'll have to show me how.'

She laughed her great laugh. 'It's easy,' she roared. 'You're lucky today. Look at the weather. This is not *le midi, mon brave.* In the *sud ouest* it can be cold and wet and then it's no fun I can tell you.'

Next to her was M. Flor who had been the Mayor of our village when we first bought the house. As he shook my hand I noticed with a sense of shock how he had aged and realised that lately I could only have seen him from a distance giving me a wave as he passed on his tractor. And the tall young man at his side must be his son Guillaume. I remembered him as a twelve-year-old, a year younger than Matthew was when we first came here. I remembered him particularly because, like our younger son, he was asthmatic. He looked bronzed and fit now as he joked with a group of young men, most of whom had the local face, dark-eyed, broad and flat with a short nose and wide, upturned mouth.

My husband Mike and I watched for a few moments before joining the lines of the pickers, one on each side of the row of vines. We saw that each *vendangeur* worked slightly ahead of the person opposite, the reason becoming quickly apparent when we started. It was necessary to thrust one's hands through the thick leaves while feeling for the stems, which were often so convoluted and strong that they were difficult to cut even with sharp secateurs. Once severed the bunches were unexpectedly heavy and pleasing to handle.

The dark-haired woman working opposite me smiled through the leaves. 'I don't think you know me,' she said, 'but my brother is the tiler. He did your kitchen floor about ten years ago. Do you remember him?'

'Of course. And I remember too that he was so pleased to do the job because, he told me, he had a sister who was a wonderful cook living nearby and he would be able to eat with her at midday.'

She laughed. 'You know where I live?'

'Yes. The house in the dip. Just past the little bridge.'

'That's the one. Why don't you call in one day when you come back from the market?'

Our baskets soon filled. The only machine in use was the oldest tractor, bought in 1947, which pulled the container into which the grapes were tipped. Those, like me, who were not strong enough to swing the heavy baskets up and over the edge had to shout *'Panier plein!'* and wait for a pair of strong brown arms to stretch through the leaves, lift the basket and return it empty. Apart from the chugging of the old tractor and the fact that our baskets were plastic, *la vendange* it seemed was much as it had been in the old days. *Autrefois* – the nostalgic expression we hear so often here. Could this be why it was so special?

At an unhurried pace we moved steadily down the rows

and the banter was continuous between the smiling mouths glimpsed through the leaves. There was much teasing and telling of bawdy jokes, many of them in Occitan or patois which made them unintelligible to me, but the laughter was infectious. Tall Mme Barrou seemed to be a constant butt and I did partly understand her description of a long ago moment of pleasure on the top of a hay cart. She laughed uproariously. '*Mon Dieu!* We were in such a hurry,' she said wiping her eyes; and, needing no help, she swung her basket up, jostling the men with her wide shoulders as she emptied it into the red container.

When it was full Raymond, *le patron*, would drive slowly up the hill to empty the load into the waiting trailer which had been scrubbed, hosed and lined with a tarpaulin kept especially for the grapes. That was our only moment of respite. Once each basket was full there was nothing to do but wait for his return. For these few moments of welcome idleness some, sighing, lowered themselves to the ground others stood and stretched, hand in the small of the back, while the young ones teased each other and chased the dogs. With a shout of '*Attention!*' Raymond trundled back, those in his path flattening themselves against the vines as he passed. We emptied the basket and began again.

Veronique, Raymond's daughter, twenty-two and unmarried, had discarded her smart office clothes and the sophisticated boredom that went with them and, in rumpled shorts and tee-shirt, giggled happily, eyeing Guillaume between the dense, blue-sprayed leaves. What romantic opportunities *la vendange* must always have provided. In the very proper act of gathering in this harvest, which of itself promised revelry and intoxication, what possibilities for eyes and hands to meet over baskets heavy with scented fruit. What chances for touching and kissing and what risks of being seen by other watchful eyes in the warm and leafy privacy between the rows. I was beginning to understand the special memories which were a part of *la vendange*.

As the sun rose higher the vines were festooned with discarded clothes and the dogs lay panting in the shadiest places. By eleven-thirty Mme Barrou began to complain that she was hungry. A great shout went up. They had clearly been expecting this.

'What's to be done?' shouted Raymond, as he inched the tractor forward. 'You should eat more breakfast.' When she had finished reciting what she had eaten that morning before joining us, that was clearly not the reason. She added darkly that a certain farmer she had heard of – she did not say precisely who – was in the habit of serving his workers a drink and cakes at eleven. There was more laughter. 'He must be English,' teased Raymond, 'They're always stopping to drink coffee.'

'I don't know anything about the English,' retorted Mme Barrou. 'All I know is that I've got a hole in my stomach like this.' She demonstrated with her big, stained fists. 'And I need a little something to put in it.'

One of the young men brought her a bunch of sweet white grapes from the far side of the vineyard and she seized them with joy, cramming them into her wide mouth. Holding them with the flat of her hand she screwed up her eyes with pleasure as the juice ran off her chin and down her apron.

Claudette, laughing, announced that she was going back to the farm to prepare the meal. She had been cooking all the previous day, the traditional dishes for the *vendangeurs*. Her mother who is in her seventies, and was looking very tired, went with her to help. Mme Barrou gazed with longing at the disappearing chef, sighed, and set to work again. Whether her hunger caused her to lose her concentration, or whether it was entirely Fernande's fault, we did not know but, shouting *'Panier plein!'* and heaving her basket over the vine Fernande lowered it with a thud onto Mme Barrou's head. Even the ox-like Mme Barrou was momentarily stunned. Everyone left their work to commiserate with her, although they, and eventually she, had to laugh.

'You should wear your crash helmet, like when you ride your Solex,' shouted someone.

Not for Mme Barrou a trendy coloured mobylette. She

persists with one of the very first forms of motorised bicycle, an old black Solex with a front wheel drive. She looked up in astonishment and indignation. *'Moi!'* she yelled, *'Je ne porte jamais de casquette, moi. Mon Solex, c'est un Solex de plein air.'* Poor Fernande apologised for the third time. Mme Barrou chose a position as far away from her as possible and we began work again, but as soon as the church bell for midday sounded across the fields she put down her basket and announced that she at least was going back to eat. We finished the last two rows to the sound of her Solex growing fainter as it carried her back to the farm.

When we drove into the courtyard there were enamel bowls of hot water and bars of crude yellow soap set out on chairs, on which Veronique was carefully arranging large linen towels as though performing some ancient ceremony. As we queued to wash our stained hands and arms wonderful smells drifted out from the long dining-room on the veranda.

The soup tureens were already on the table and beside each place was poured an aperitif of *vin de noix*.

'Fabrication maison,' said Claudette and we toasted each other: *'À la vôtre,'* with the traditional response *'À la tienne Etienne.'*

It was like a party, but of relaxed revellers with sweaty faces and dirty clothes. The *vin de noix* was two years old. Claudette had marinated a hundred walnut leaves and three sliced nuts in a litre of *eau-de-vie* for two months. She had then discarded the leaves and nuts and diluted each wine glass of *eau-de-vie* with a litre of good red wine, sweetened with 150 grammes of sugar. It was delicious.

Mme Barrou drained hers in one gulp and reached for a slice of bread from the piles on the table. The soup was ladled out and the meal began. The young men were ravenous and the beautifully arranged plates of hors d'oeuvre which followed – hard boiled eggs with dark golden yolks, crimson tomatoes from the field, huge sweet onions and sliced cucumbers – were quickly demolished as the first wine, the local *vin de table*, was poured.

11

Great dishes of the traditional *pot-au-feu*; chicken, whole sweet carrots and a yellow stuffing made with bread, garlic and egg yolks, were similarly treated while the mounds of bread were constantly replenished. Next Claudette brought in dishes of sizzling macaroni in a bechamel sauce topped with cheese and gradually the pace of the eating slackened. Even the young men refused a second helping. Guillaume apologised.

'Well – we all ate so much yesterday,' he grinned.'

Claudette looked disappointed. 'It's true,' she said sadly.

I realised that this was the third day of *la vendange* in our commune. The third day of comparable meals, and the roast was yet to come. Claudette shrugged. She had cooked it so she was certainly going to serve it, and at least Mme Barrou had lost none of her appetite. Her great fists clutching her knife and fork she attacked everything as if it might escape from her plate.

With the succulent slices of veal Raymond produced bottles of *Vieux Cahors* which were savoured and approved. Naturally we had to eat a little salad to cleanse the palate and then a little fruit to finish and it was three o'clock before we started work again, this time in a vineyard closer to the farm.

We were all somewhat sluggish and it was Grandpa, who celebrated his eightieth birthday this summer and had been at market all morning, who put us to shame. He stood high on the tractor and emptied the baskets one after the other.

'Does this remind you of your youth?' someone asked. He shrugged and laughed but said nothing.

Mme Barrou also was strangely quiet. 'She's no use in the afternoons,' muttered Raymond. 'You watch, she'll be having a snooze before long.' Sure enough, while we waited for the container to be emptied I saw her stretched out, her back against a cherry tree and her mouth open. She woke when the tractor returned but after a little while she gave up and went home.

The *Cave Coopérative*, after sampling the local grapes, had decided that the first three days' harvest would be used to

12

make *vin ordinaire*, and so we picked both red and white grapes. The white, *Sauvignon Blanc* and *Semillon*, were much more difficult to see as they are almost the same colour as the sun bleached leaves. Mme Barrou was replaced by the village mechanic, his wife and six-year-old son. The mechanic said he had been busy mending a tractor all morning but now he was free to lend a hand. The only time his little boy stopped chattering or singing in a thin, high voice was when his mouth was crammed with grapes.

By six o'clock we had finished. The light was beginning to fade and the loaded trailers had yet to be taken to the *Cave Coopérative*, eight kilometres away. An escort would be needed for the return journey along the dark winding road as the headlamps on the tractors were feeble and there were no rear lights on the trailers. As Claudette was busy preparing yet more food I volunteered to go; just to sit in the comfort of the car was an unexpected pleasure.

Outside the *Cave des Sept Monts* I watched the farmers come and go, and tired-looking young men manoeuvred their fork-lifts between the long rows of tall, green-painted metal bins, the proprietors' names chalked on the sides. Black and white grapes filled the dark red interiors and the smell of fruit was overpowering. There was a constant hum of machinery and outside, like a rearing dinosaur, a mounting conveyor belt spewed out stalks and pips into an already overflowing trailer.

I crossed the road and sat on the bank waiting for the tractors. Our three turned the bend with my husband leading, grinning broadly. He always enjoys driving the tractor and, clearly, carrying the grapes to be made into the wine which he so loves to drink was a special pleasure. One after the other our trailers were backed up and emptied. We watched the mass of grapes tipped up and up until they fell into the great red painted maw below to be churned and crushed by the giant screw. Away they went to become just a small part of the *vin ordinaire* for 1988. The recorded weight came up on the dial and then we waited for the all important alcohol content. It was 12% and Raymond was content.

Outside it was very dark. In the beam of my headlights the tractors swung their empty trailers out one behind the other into the narrow road. Slowly I drove behind them, illuminating the trundling convoy. Their one visible light was a revolving yellow lamp high up on a pole at the rear of the tractor seat and its hypnotic effect and my fatigue made it hard to stay awake as, followed by the occasional motorist impatient to overtake, we wound slowly homeward.

At supper Grandpa was the liveliest I had seen him all summer. 'It does me good a bit of exercise like that,' he shouted. 'A bit of twisting and turning and lifting. Otherwise I'm always bent forward.' I wondered whether he would be stiff the following day, but the next morning I saw him in the distance, his gun over his shoulder, striding down across the field, the dogs at his heels.

It was another glorious morning. Was October always like this? Probably not. One thing we have learned is that the weather here can be unpredictable but the sun is much stronger than in England and that is, after all, why we came. That morning there was a warm wind blowing from the south – *le Vent d'Autan* they call it here. After breakfast I took my chair round onto the south-facing terrace. It was Sunday and there was no sound apart from the sighing of the wind blowing across empty fields. Yet without moving my head I could see so many creatures. A cricket bent a blade of grass as it climbed, a lizard basked on a stone at my feet. A miner bee backed out of her perfectly cylindrical hole, tidying it before flying off in search of food. A swarm of newly hatched ants was being shepherded by what looked like six large winged prefects and small red and black insects ran up the stems of the hollyhocks and into the seed pods. A daddy-long-legs tottered across the grass on high heels and suddenly a tree frog called from the honeysuckle behind me.

If only there were more birds like the thrushes and blackbirds that I see in my London garden. Here they shoot them all. The only birds that are safe are the tits, swallows, woodpeckers and buzzards, for they are inedible. Yet I once heard Grandpa discussing magpie soup which he had eaten as a child.

'What about crow soup?' someone asked.

'Not bad,' he replied, 'but the skin is tough.'

The children grimaced. 'We were poor,' he shouted, 'we had to eat what there was.'

Now he and Grandma are comfortable. State pensions are more generous here than in England and the old couple only work because they have always done so. Each year when we leave we wonder whether they will survive the winter. Grandma is particularly frail and her eyes are not good. When we first came she was always planting things for me in the garden; shrubs and bulbs and sprigs of broom that she dug up in the woods. Now she often just sits and dreams and her tiny feet shuffle when she walks.

I left my chair and walked through the house to the other side. Standing under the wide porch I could see someone else with a gun emerging from the edge of the wood high up under the hill. There's nothing left to shoot but they love to dress up and pretend and on a morning like this who could blame them? Tomorrow we would harvest the last of the grapes and then close the house, hand the keys to Raymond and leave for England.

2

*I*t was late in the long, hot, dry summer of '76 when we first found our house in the sun. Semi-derelict and quite overgrown, it had been on the market for three summers and no one had lived in it for eleven years. I like to think that it was waiting for us. My husband Mike and I are lizards. Normally workaholics, when the sun is strong and the air warm our only urgency is to bask. I once briefly contemplated marriage with a handsome, fair-skinned young man with whom I imagined myself in love until, on a day trip to the sea, he covered his splendid legs with a towel in case they burned and I knew that he was not for me.

Each summer we would drive our two sons as far south as time and money would allow. We would all idly dream of buying a house in Italy or Spain even though we knew we could not afford it. It was not until we went to the south west of France where we discovered old houses, abandoned and not expensive – the French much preferring to build smart new villas – that we realised for the first time that our dream might just become reality. In Lot-et-Garonne we fell in love with a region of small undulating farms, medieval hill-top towns, their balconies crammed with flowers, incredibly cheap, gastronomic menus and simple, friendly people. Even then it was to take us five years to find what we wanted.

Each holiday we would point the car south west from Calais. The search was on and it filled a need in me for something to absorb me completely. Ever since I had finished playing at the Piccadilly Theatre in 'Man of La Mancha' I had felt a great restlessness. Musical roles like Dulcinea in the story of Don Quixote are once in a lifetime and I had been incredibly lucky to get it – and even luckier to repeat it the following summer playing opposite Richard Kiley who had created the role on Broadway. The notices made my agent happy.

It was a special show. The distinguished critic of the *New York Times*, Brooks Atkinson wrote: 'In the final scene Dulcinea and Don Quixote are not figures of fun but enlightened human beings who know something private but beautiful that is outside the range of ordinary experience.' Small wonder that I found the world of cabaret and one-nighters to which I had returned less than satisfying.

Looking for our house in the sun became almost an obsession and in the next five years we must have seen scores of houses. We looked at complete ruins, converted or unconverted barns, neatly restored villas, even shacks made of wattle and daub which looked as though a high wind would blow them away, but we found nothing that was exactly right. And of course each year when we returned our slowly growing savings were outstripped by rising prices. Would we ever find the right house in the right location at a price we could afford?

That summer we had almost been persuaded by an English entrepreneur, living in the south west, to buy a huge barn that he had found and to let him supervise the conversion. Still undecided we went to have another look. The interior was huge. The walls of beautiful, honey-coloured stone were a metre thick and the original wooden stalls still full of hay. However, one wall needed to come down and be completely rebuilt, it was too close to the road and the distant view was marred by a giant pylon. But it was, not surprisingly, very cheap and our holiday was almost over. Could we bear to go home once more disappointed? That night we lay awake.

'Is *that* what we've really been looking for?' asked Mike.

'No.' I had to admit it. And that was that.

We decided to forget the wretched barn and spend just one more day searching. We had gradually established priorities and the first had to be the one thing which we could not change – the location. Next morning at an agency that we had not tried before we explained, as best we could, what it was that we were looking for. The agent, a plump, dishevelled blonde, seemed sympathetic and armed with her list of three possibilities we set off yet again. The first house turned out to be a sagging wooden cabin in a gloomy valley. We did not even stop. So much for her understanding. It was no good, we might as well start thinking about going back to England. Even the intrepid Matthew was getting fed up with all this fruitless house-hunting.

It was midday. We looked at the second name on the list and consulted our, by now, dog-eared map. The owner, a M. Bertrand, lived in a farm on the edge of a village about six kilometres away. We might as well just go and look. We could, perhaps, eat our picnic in the village square and buy a drink at the café. As we approached the village – hardly even that: a shop, a church, two petrol pumps with an urn of oleanders on either side and a telephone box under a tree – nothing moved. It appeared deserted. We climbed out of the van into the midday heat and looked about us. The stillness was broken by the creak of a gate and turning we saw a very small, very old woman in a dark speckled pinafore and carpet slippers coming silently towards us. Did she by any chance know M. Bertrand, the farmer, we asked her? She smiled, raising her thin eyebrows.

'*Mais, bien sûr Monsieur,*' she whispered, pointing down the road ahead. We did not know then of course, that she had known him for forty years and others in the village for twice as long.

Several tethered dogs barked wildly as we drove into the farmyard. The house was quite imposing and the garden ablaze with asters and zinnias. A boy about the same age as Matthew came out of a side door. He had long brown legs, a smiling intelligent face and he explained that his father was '*en train de manger*'. We apologised for we knew, even then, that there could hardly be a greater crime than interrupting a Frenchman's meal, especially at midday.

'We'll come back later,' we said, but at that moment M. Bertrand himself appeared, wiping his greasy chin with the back of his hand. He was small but sturdy, dark-eyed, his sunburnt feet in dusty espadrilles. We apologised for disturbing him but he shook his head and smiled. It was nothing. Yes, he did have a house for sale, he would be glad to show it to us. He climbed onto a small motorcycle. We protested. It was always slightly embarrassing to have to explain to any vendor that their house was really very charming but not exactly what was required – and to have to do so after dragging this poor man from his meal!

'If you'll just tell us how to get there,' we pleaded, 'we'll go and look and then, if we are interested, we'll call back.'

He smiled at us, shaking his head.

'Impossible,' he said. 'You'd never find it.'

It was at that moment that we had our first stirrings of excitement.

'Is it well situated?' asked Mike.

'Better than here,' he yelled over the sudden roar of the bike and away he careered down the drive. We followed.

Two hundred yards along the winding, narrow road he suddenly disappeared from view as he turned to the right up a rough track and we turned, bumping and swaying behind him. The track swung left, climbing and narrowing through dry, head-high maize. At the far end of this tunnel we could just glimpse two ruined walls and a great heap of stones. Our hearts sank. Was that it? The farmer, no doubt realising what we were thinking, turned and, pointing at the ruin, shook his head, the bike lurching wildly. Another turn, this time to the right, past a dried-up pond and a large barn and as he stopped, we saw our house for the first time.

The engines switched off, the sudden stillness was overwhelming as we climbed down into the dry, bleached grass. As our ears adjusted we became aware of the papery rustling of the maize and the shrilling of crickets in the dry, sweet air. It was very hot although the sun was obscured by thin cloud and as we walked toward the house we all spoke quietly as though someone were asleep.

It was a long, low building and, from what seemed to be the front, which I now know is the back, it appeared featureless. The end section on the right seemed to be an afterthought, having been roofed in different tiles from the ancient Roman ones which slithered down the remainder of the roof.

'That part is not so old,' said M. Bertrand. 'Not quite a hundred years I think.'

'And the rest?' I enquired.

He shrugged. 'Two hundred, three hundred, perhaps more. Who knows?' He led us round the side of the house where a long-neglected vine had interwoven with a japonica bush. It had climbed higher than the roof and then twisted over to form a long, shady, ragged tunnel full of spiders' webs.

The real front of the house now came into view. The nearest corner was almost hidden by what had probably once been a neat box hedge but was now a tall, straggling screen of trees. Beyond this the roof sloped steeply down to form a wide porch. Behind two low iron gates of uneven width we could see a stone well, an ancient front door and a collection of cobwebbed clutter; lengths of string and wire posts and broomhandles and cracked clay pots. M. Bertrand

N

shooed away the cows which grazed right up to the porch
and taking out a huge key on a tattered shred of dark red
cloth, he unlocked the door.

Stepping into that cool, dark interior was the strangest
experience for the furniture was still there, layered with dust
and cobwebs as if in a fairy tale; yet even after all those years
of neglect I still felt the strong sense of its having been loved
and cared for. M. Bertrand pushed the shutters open and
the fierce light flooded in through the grimy glass showing
more clearly the long table, rickety chairs, and a sideboard,
dark and massive with an old lady's straw hat lying on the
top. I picked it up and slowly put it on and I knew then
that this was the house I wanted. Something about
continuity; impossible to explain.

In this main room, to the side of the one small, deep-set
window were two tiny wood-burning stoves. Their sooty
chimney pipes crossed the greasy wall to join the main
chimney breast of the wide, open fire-place, the hearth a
simple iron plate on the floor. An opening to the left led
to the newer part of the house which consisted of two quite

large rooms opening off this main room. M. Bertrand opened one door then another.

'*Attention!*' he shouted as we began to follow him. We soon saw why. Unlike the first room which had a cement floor, these were wooden but, alas, now almost entirely eaten away. As he swung the shutter open I shrieked as an outraged bat flew from its home between the joists, skimming my face as it hurtled out of doors.

Mike, always more practical than I, was looking very doubtful. 'It'll all have to be completely re-done,' he muttered as we went back into the main room and looked up at the ceiling, where there were several large holes giving glimpses of the sky. Green trails of lichen on the corner wall showed where the rain had trickled in over the years. My heart sank. The specification had indeed said '*INTERIEUR A RESTORER*' but . . .

Another two doors led off to the right, the first into a corridor about nine feet wide. There were ominous holes in the beaten earth floor which was strewn with broken rabbit hutches, wire cages, dozens of empty bottles, and everywhere cobwebs on the cobwebs, layered with dust like thick muslin. Matthew, always ahead, had already found a mouldering, uneven staircase at the far end lit by a very small window. Above this was another, even older window with no frame or glass, just a hand-carved stone opening, closed by a crude, heavy oak shutter which, when we opened it inwards, showered us with dust but revealed wonderful old nails with which it was studded. There was enough light for us to gingerly ascend into the attic or *grenier* which ran the whole length of the house. It was not in as bad a state as we had expected and was full of old farm implements, piles of corn husks, old boxes and even what looked like another ancient sideboard in the far corner.

Downstairs once more in the main room we opened the second door on the right and found a small room with an unusually low, tongued and grooved pine ceiling and a glass door which led outside. M. Bertrand explained that this room was the newest addition. It had been built inside the main structure for the old lady who had lived there with her son, because it was south facing and so warmer in the winter.

'How old was she?' I asked.

'Ninety-two when she died,' he answered, 'and her son almost seventy.'

The last area M. Bertrand showed us was the huge outhouse or *chai* which was, he told us, a store for wine, north facing but not like a *cave*, which is below ground. We went in through a wide oak door at one side of the porch. About eighteen feet high nearest to the house, it sloped steeply down to barely five feet at the far end. 'Brilliant!' breathed Matthew as we stepped inside. Not only dust and cobwebs here but also an eleven years' old collection of dead leaves from the two overhanging ash trees. Along the lowest wall, raised on two heavy beams were a dozen large oak barrels and several smaller ones. there was a pair of ancient scales with weights; a weird, wooden, wheelbarrow-like machine which was, we learned, for winnowing the wheat and another for stripping the corn from the cob; benches, baskets, lanterns, boxes, besoms and yet more bottles.

We wanted to talk about the house. Mike explained to M. Bertrand that we had a picnic with us in our camping van. Might we eat it there by the house? We were sure that he too might like to finish his own meal. We were very interested. (Very interested? I was besotted!) We would stay there until he returned.

His reaction surprised us. His face fell. He pushed his straw hat back off his brown forehead to show the white strip beneath. He shrugged and blushed, shifting his brown feet in the dust. What could be the problem? Eventually he explained that the previous summer he had done precisely that with another group of people. On his return they had already left, taking with them the old brass lamp which had hung above the table. What could we say? We suggested he lock the house but he suddenly smiled, shook our hands and disappeared in a cloud of smoke.

Once more the silence descended as we gazed at the neglected house. Many of the ancient tiles had slipped and staggered down the steep slope of the roof giving it a drunken look. The plaster on the thick walls was stained and crumbling, the shutters falling to pieces and holes in the ceiling – but how I wanted it.

I handed out the bread, cheese and fruit and Mike uncorked the wine. Too excited to sit down, we circled the house again, picnic in hand. Matthew discovered two small outhouses that looked as though they might have been pigsties and another with a curiously high, narrow double door and a copper set into the end wall. There was also a second porch closed in with ugly galvanised doors on the west side which faced the barn. There was no mention of the barn on the specification so we assumed that the farmer used it and it was indeed full of hay. How much land would be ours? It said 2000 square metres but as we were surrounded by fields, it did not seem too important. The pale cows watched us, standing in a line. Mike poured himself another glass. Might this be the moment to try to explain how I felt? Before I had time to say anything Matthew came hurtling back again.

'It's great. We can have it Dad, can't we?' he said.

His father looked at him, glass in hand. 'I think we might. There's an awful lot to do, it's in a dreadful state and you'll have to help, you realise. But I feel it's manageable and it's less than five thousand pounds.' We were home and dry.

By the time M. Bertrand returned we were planning which would be the main bedroom, which the kitchen, and Matthew had already chosen for himself the floorless room facing south. I now realise that he was the only one who got it right but we had not lived in our house then. We hadn't even bought it.

M. Bertrand seemed delighted. We shook hands again and then it was a matter of returning to the Agency to pay a deposit and sign the agreement. It seemed a comparatively simple procedure.

'There's another way back to the road,' said M. Bertrand.

'It will be quicker for you. Go down that track,' he shouted, pointing, and then he whizzed away. Ten minutes later we were completely lost in a strange farmyard encircled by dogs, cats, chicken, ducks and guinea fowl and a family of three generations who had come out to show us the track that we should have taken. Our new home was certainly remote.

In order to pay the deposit and, more important it seemed, the Agent's commission which was, we discovered in our region, six per cent and, alas, *à la charge de l'acheteur*, we spent the next hour chasing from one bank to another. At that time one could only write a sterling cheque for fifty pounds cash so the process had to be repeated in each available bank. Fortunately the small town appeared to be full of banks. Returning to the Agency we struggled to make sense of the official documents. Mike, who many years before as an eighteen-year-old soldier in wartime France and the only one in his squadron with any French, had had a great deal of practice but nevertheless found it hard going. My own French was abysmally rusty and Matthew, who could just about conjugate *avoir* and *être* if he put his mind to it soon got bored and went to have a snooze in the van.

We were almost finished when we were joined by a newly bathed and dressed M. Bertrand and his small, fair, girlish wife. With a wide face and a radiant smile she was clearly enjoying this unexpected trip into town. At last the documents were completed and we could all leave the airless office for a drink at the café across the road.

'Tomorrow I must get the *géomètre* to measure your land exactly,' said M. Bertrand, and we arranged to meet at the house the following day. We toasted our new friendship in Pernod and Dubonnet. Clinking our glasses we beamed at each other. Time would tell us the quality of these friends that we had had the good fortune to find.

Le Géomètre was young, handsome and very serious. He walked round our house to the front porch and regarded it in silence for several minutes. Then he said solemnly, '*Oui.*

C'est très recherché.' We were suitably pleased. We thought so too.

He paced and measured, M. Bertrand following him banging in small wooden stakes at each corner. The narrow strip of land between the barn and the house was evenly divided and then he marched off along the track with his giant tape measure. The further he went the further fell M. Bertrand's face. We were to learn over the years that our friend is totally without guile, his face mirrors each succeeding thought. Then we only saw that he had not realised quite how much of his meadow would soon be ours. We watched the graceful young man pace onward. 'Right!' shouted Mike. 'That's plenty.'

M. Bertrand looked surprised but extremely relieved. 'Are you sure?' he asked.

'Sure,' we nodded. We knew that it would be a long time before we would worry about the size of a garden, there was so much to be done on the house. So the stakes were hammered in and *Le Géomètre* disappeared slowly down the track in his elegant car. A man of taste. He knew something *recherché* when he saw it.

So with our holiday at an end we took our last look at our house. We were a little disconcerted to learn that it was called *Bel-Air*. A name with such a smart, trans-Atlantic connotation seemed singularly inappropriate for our neglected and unpretentious dwelling. M. Bertrand explained that within a few kilometres there were four ancient houses all called *Grèze Longue* and that *grèze* was a kind of chalky soil. There were *Grèze Longue Haut* and *Bas* for obvious reasons, *Au Bosc de Grèze Longue* because it was in a wood and our house was actually called *Bel-Air de Grèze Longue* because we had the best view and caught all the fresh air. That made it much more acceptable.

Excited as we were there was nothing more to do but return to England and dream about it. Until the transaction was completed we could not begin any alterations. We took a few inadequate photographs to show Adam, our eldest son, who was somewhere in Europe touring with a pop group. In London we had to apply to the Bank of England for permission to buy abroad and we also had to pay the iniquitous dollar premium which was, in 1976, 45%, for the privilege of spending our own money on which we had already paid tax!

In October we received a letter from the lawyer, or *notaire*, saying that our agreement would be even more delayed. When *le géomètre* had consulted the ancient map he had discovered that at some time in the past M. Bertrand, in order that his cows should have easier access to the pond, had simply altered the position of the track or *chemin rural* which passed our house. This explained why it now ran past the back, rather than the front door as it had originally done. Such an alteration was, it appeared, strictly forbidden and French bureaucracy now required the passing of a special *acte* by the commune. We could only imagine M. Bertrand's face when he heard this piece of news!

3

By the end of November the contracts were ready to be signed. As we also wanted to contact a local builder to at least begin those urgent tasks which were beyond us, namely the roof and the dangerous floors, we decided on a brief, weekend trip to France. On a cold Thursday evening we set out for Newhaven. The rain lashed the side of the van all the way from London and by the time we reached the coast the wind had risen. As we drove through customs there was a loud bang as the rocket announced the launching of the life boat. The next hour and a half was spent swaying up and down on board the ferry as we waited for a tug to pull us out of harbour against a force-ten gale. It did not seem a propitious start.

Landing at Dieppe after midnight we drove until four in the morning when we tried to sleep in a lay-by. The passing headlights of early lorries soon made sleep impossible and we continued our journey through the relentless rain. France had never seemed such a huge country. We lost our way more than once in unfamiliar towns and it was almost seven in the evening and with a thick mist closing in when we drove into Villereal, a small, medieval town about twenty kilometres from our house. We could go no further.

Exhausted, we pulled up in front of the hotel in the square and climbed stiffly down from the van. It had at last stopped raining. The soft air, warmer than in London, was scented with the smoke from the wood fires which burned in the sleepy houses. The church clock chimed the hour. We looked slowly round at a view which, apart from the television aerials, had hardly changed in six hundred years and we knew why we had made this long, wet journey.

After a restoring bath and a drink we telephoned M. Bertrand. 'Where are you?' he asked.

'At Villereal. In the hotel.'

'But your room is all ready for you – here – with us!' he cried. But he understood when we explained our fatigue. Even the idea of crossing the dreaded channel made him shudder. We promised to be with him the following morning and we were so tired that even the effort of that short conversation was enough. We were quite glad not to have to continue in French for the rest of the evening. It was in a blissful silence that we enjoyed the oysters which followed the soup.

Our first call next morning was to Maître Fournon, the *notaire*. A great rugby enthusiast, he enlivens his office with dozens of trophies and photographs of stalwart teams with folded arms. The documents duly signed he told us that we still could not have a copy of the deeds until after the final redrawing of the map to include the changed *chemin rural*. How long would that take? He gave a Gallic shrug and advised us to forget about it until we came at Easter.

Now for our village and M. Bertrand. We drove up to the farm, automatically turning left round the raised lawn shaded by high elms.

'Everyone else goes round the other way,' he teased as he came out to greet us with his wife. Mme Bertrand wore thick stockings, and a woollen cardigan over her flowered overall but her wonderful smile was the same. M. Bertrand had the addresses of a *charpentier* for the roof and a *maçon* to do the floors. We soon began to appreciate the demarcations. Off we drove again. There was so much to be packed into that day as we had to be back in London the following night. Looking back on it I marvel at our energy, but that was twelve years ago!

The *charpentier*, tall and somewhat lugubrious, was not sure that he would be able to manage our roof before Easter but the *maçon*, older and broader with a round flat face, in which his mischievous eyes looked like currants in a bun, promised that our floors would be done. He suggested that he take away all the rotten wooden flooring and replace it with cement which could be tiled at a later date. He laughed a lot and spoke so fast in his strong South West accent that we could barely understand him but he and M. Bertrand had been schoolboys together and we felt that all would be well.

That evening we were invited to supper at the farm and we met the rest of the family. M. Bertrand's parents-in-law, to whom the farm had originally belonged, lived separately in an adjoining, small house, but all meals were *en famille*. We were formally introduced. M. and Mme Meligny were both small and slender but wiry with rough, strong hands and weather-beaten faces. M. Meligny had shrewd blue eyes and a surprisingly loud, resonant voice, and when his wife smiled her rather solemn face lit up just as her daughter's did. Philippe, the boy we had seen on our first visit, brought his ten-year-old sister to meet us. Veronique was plump and shy and said nothing but gazed at us all the time with large dark eyes while her brother tried a few words of English in a clear and precise accent. The whole family were impressed when we obviously understood him.

Before eating we were invited to tour the farm; M. Bertrand was clearly keen to show us everything. In the first barn adjoining the house we admired his herd of massive, cream-coloured cows, called, we were told, *Blondes d'Aquitaine*. Next door we threw scraps to three great snorting, squealing pigs who ran out of their sties at the sound of our voices. We helped Veronique and her mother

31

to shut up the dozens of chickens, ducks, guinea fowl and turkeys that range freely during the day. We saw cages of quail and rabbits and M. Bertrand pointed out his plum orchards, two quite close to the farm and another just visible on a distant hillside. The fourth, he told us, was nearer to Bel-Air and we would be able to enjoy the blossom when we came at Easter. We saw the the tall shed for drying the tobacco and as we returned to the house Mme Meligny came down the steps carrying a steaming bucket.

'Ah,' he said eagerly. 'You'll find this interesting.' Innocently we followed. 'We are fattening these ducks for *foie gras*,' he said. There in one corner of the barn behind a low wooden barrier were twelve fat ducks and a small stool. I was completely unprepared for this and not at all sure that I wanted to watch. Yet what an opportunity to see for myself! He laughed at the expression on my face. '*Venez. Venez voir*,' he said kindly.

Mme Meligny took her first duck firmly and holding it between her knees she carefully put a funnel down its throat, all the while stroking it and talking softly. She put a handful of the warm maize into the funnel which had a handle like a baby mouli and slowly the feed was forced down the duck's throat. Another handful disappeared into the duck who was then released. It staggered back into the corner and sat down ruffling its feathers. The others quacked and fluttered but, I had to admit, made little protest when their turn came. The origin for *foie gras* was, they told me, the result of the natural gorging of ducks on ripe figs which made their livers both larger and tastier. '*C'est du travail*,' the old lady said. 'It's a lot of work. Twice a day for eight weeks.' She finished the last bird and we went in to supper leaving the ducks quacking softly as the barn door closed.

In the farm kitchen delicious smells greeted us. This splendid meal, the first of so many at this long table, began with pumpkin soup, *soupe de potiron*, golden and warming. This was followed by slices of home-cured ham and tiny gherkins, with dishes of butter for the bread. Next came an enormous stew of tender veal with carrots which was so good that we made the fatal mistake of allowing ourselves to be persuaded to take second helpings, imagining, not altogether unreasonably, that this was the main course. We drank a light red wine made on the farm.

'*Ce n'est qu'un petit vin*' smiled M. Bertrand. He asked how much a litre of such wine would cost in London and his eyes opened ever wider as we estimated.

They asked us so many questions. They wanted to know about the English weather, what we thought of the Common Market, what it was like to live in London and all the details of our families. We were clearly objects of great interest. They wanted to know where in France Mike had been as a young soldier and we learned that for the first five years of his daughter's life M. Meligny had been a prisoner of war in Germany. 'How did you manage then?' we asked the old lady.

She shrugged and smiled. 'It was hard,' she said, 'but in the country you help one another – *c'est normal.*'

I was curious about our predecessor at Bel-Air. Her name I learned was Mme Costes; they called her Anaïs.

'*Anaïs* was the mother and *Alaïs* her son,' said M. Bertrand emphasising the difference. He spoke slowly and clearly and watched my face intently to make sure that I understood.

'How long had she lived there?'

'I'm not sure,' he replied.

'She was already there when I came here to be married,' said Mme Meligny, 'And that was nearly fifty years ago. She was *vaillante*. Her son was handicapped after he caught polio and her husband died suddenly when she was in her forties. Poor Anaïs. There's an old photograph of her somewhere. I'll see if I can find it for the next time you come.'

Replete and contented we were astonished to see Mme Bertrand carrying in two dishes, one of roast pork, the other of chicken and bowls of French beans. We had, of course, to try some and anyway it smelled so good. M. Bertrand was carefully filtering the darkest wine that I had ever seen from a dusty, unlabelled bottle which was to be our first introduction to the *vin noir de Cahors*. This especially dark wine from a local grape is grown in the rich red-brown soil which slopes down to the river Lot near Cahors. These factors, combined with the climate and an ancient method of production, give the wine a very high tannin content and its unique colour. In 1971 it was accorded an *appellation contrôlée*; this long overdue elevation, according to M. Bertrand, was chiefly due to its popularity with M. Pompidou. I must say I share his taste.

A simple green salad was followed by a selection of cheeses and then, as the coffee was poured, Mme Meligny brought in a plate piled high with still warm small yellow pancakes, rather like Scottish bannocks. These too were made with pumpkins. *'C'est la saison du potiron,'* laughed the old lady. We ate and drank far too much that evening. It was all so wonderful and strange and yet, there was also a sense of homecoming. We slept that night in a high wooden bed with rough linen sheets in Veronique's room, filled with dolls, and were woken next morning by the shattering cry of the cockerel under the window.

It was with thick heads and uncertain stomachs that we said our farewells. London seemed a million miles away. I remember almost nothing of the return journey apart from the strange things that slid about in the back of the van; a tall, wicker-covered *bonbonne* which held twenty litres of M. Bertrand's *petit vin*, a great bouquet of chinese lanterns and silver honesty and the largest pumpkin I had ever seen.

On the last day of the year we received a letter from M. Bertrand addressed to *chers tous*. He wished us health and happiness for the coming year. He had, he said, been in touch with both the water board and the insurance man on our behalf. Water in France is metered. Although there was piped water up to Bel-Air it had never been connected. Anaïs and her son, presumably unable to afford it, had continued to haul it up from the well. M. Bertrand promised to arrange for us to have a simple outside tap before our return. As for the redrawing of the map to include the changed *chemin* he wrote:

Enfin c'est terminé et Bel-Air est bien à vous!

4

We spent the next few months collecting things to take to Bel-Air at Easter. As far as possible we wanted everything to match the feel of the house. I scoured street markets and jumble sales for odd pieces of Victorian china and unstripped pine furniture which, at the time, one could still buy cheaply. As our only running water would be an outside tap we also needed buckets and washing-up bowls and, most important, a camping lavatory and tent.

We could, of course, cook in our van but I was delighted to find in a government surplus shop a large, ex-army dixie. 'Don't get much call for these,' said the assistant climbing up to reach it, 'apart from the odd gypsy that is.' I remembered that there was a hook and chain for just such a pot in my wide black chimney. We bought enamel water pitchers and flowered jugs and basins to wash in, reminding me of my country childhood. 'Don't forget to put the cold water in first or you'll crack the basin', I could hear my mother saying. We were excited at the thought of the primitive few weeks ahead and impatient for Easter to arrive.

'Can I take Durrell?' begged Matthew. We decided that
the extra and precious space taken up by Matthew's friend
Durrell would be more than compensated for by his
unfailingly cheerful company. The night before we left we
packed our camper to the roof, packing and repacking it
several times, each time squeezing in yet one more thing.
We took two wooden armchairs, a small cupboard, rush
matting, a step ladder and white paint, mattresses and
bedding and, a last minute bargain at auction, a pine
seaman's chest with G. GUNN painted on the lid. How
many journeys had that already made we wondered. The
only spaces were two slits into which, letter-like, the boys
were to be posted.

'Crikey,' they said. 'Do we have to lie down all the
way?' We reminded them that we were to drive through
the night but we promised to stop every two hours once
it got light.

It was another wet journey. At Dieppe the customs men
took one amused look at our crammed vehicle and waved
us through. By three in the morning we had reached a
deserted Chartres where we clambered out to stretch our
legs, drank coffee in the lee of the great cathedral and gazed
in wonder at the magnificent doorway with its serene,
elongated figures. On we drove into the rain, joking about
buying our house to enjoy more sun, but nothing could
dampen our spirits as the wet slates of northern France gave
way eventually to the red Roman tiles of the south.

In bar after bar – which sold, to the giggling delight of
the boys, a fizzy drink called *pschitt* – we played
innumerable games of *le foot*, a table football, which kept
them happy. By late afternoon, weary but triumphant, we
drove into M. Bertrand's courtyard. Still it rained.

'I see you've brought some English weather with you!'
he joked, emerging in waterproof cape and hat to hand us
our key. As we drove slowly up the long track to the house,
the mud spattering the white sides of the van, we leaned
out, filling our lungs with the fresh, damp air, straining for
our first glimpse of Bel-Air. As we climbed up to the last

38

bend the wheels spun helplessly before finally getting a grip on the stones beneath the soft mud.

'If this rain doesn't stop soon this track will be impassable,' warned Mike, but I was not listening. There it was. Our house, but looking so sad and wet. The bun-faced builder was there with three workmen. I suspect that M. Bertrand must have warned them of our imminent arrival for they had just finished cementing the bedroom floors. The porch was piled high with all the old, rotten floorboards and joists. We looked slowly round the gloomy main room, so very different from our first view on that baking August day, while the rain dripped incessantly from the roof behind us in a cold wet curtain.

'We'd better try lighting the fire,' said Mike. 'If the chimney's not working it looks as though we'll have to find an hotel.' The boys protested and we all helped to lay a fire on the iron plate in the hearth. We broke up some of the old rabbit hutches in the earth-floored corridor and carried in the most worm-eaten of the floorboards. This was the moment of truth. Did the chimney work? The builders came to watch. There were a few splutters, a crackle and then a bright tongue of flame licked confidently upward and within minutes we had a blaze so glorious that we were backing away from the heat. We cheered, opened a bottle and felt ready for anything.

Once we had unloaded the van we could make up our bed but the boys insisted on sleeping in the house. They chose the smallest south-facing room with the garden door – at least it had no holes in the ceiling, other than those made by legions of woodworm. We carried in their mattresses after putting down plastic sheets. They were cautioned about the candles, but they refused torches as not being right for the house. And so we spent our first night at Bel-Air – and still it rained. In the next few days, squelching across to the lavatory which was in six inches of water began to lose its novelty; but there was worse to come.

The moment I awoke on Easter Sunday morning I was

aware of a change in the light. Sitting up to wipe a space in the steamed up window of the van I cursed as I clumsily overturned a glass of water. I need not have worried for the contents were frozen solid. Bewildered I looked out on a landscape covered in snow. We could only laugh as, clutching our Easter gifts, we later trudged across the slushy fields down to the farm where we had been invited to lunch.

How wonderful it was to be welcomed into that warm kitchen filled with the smell of good things to eat. They told us that snow was rare at any time and completely unheard of at Easter. *'Jamais! Jamais de ma vie,'* cried M. Meligny, returning from his Sunday morning card game at the café where no-one could remember such an event.

M. Bertrand, his children and his mother-in-law (*ma belle-mère* as he called her – how much more gallant a name) had all been to Mass and wore their Sunday clothes. Veronique handed round peanuts shyly as we drank our aperitifs – Pernod for the men, and for the women, my first taste of the *Vin de Noix*, the home-made fortified wine flavoured with walnuts. In the inner kitchen Mme Bertrand and her mother, now wrapped in her usual flowered overall, scurried back and forth, cutting, stirring and sprinkling. Finally came the call. *'Allez! Allez à la soupe!'* and a great tureen was carried in. Grandpa took the head of the table with M. Bertrand on his right. Mike was invited to sit on his left and I beside him. The children sat opposite each other wriggling in anticipation and Madame and her mother sat at the far end.

'Servez vous! Servez vous!' insisted Mme Bertrand.

'Come on Mum!' implored Matthew, and thus began the tradition that I serve the soup whenever I am there. In vain we warned the boys against taking second helpings. One bowl of the tasty chicken broth with noodles was swiftly followed by another. After the soup came an hors d'oeuvre of tuna fish, hard boiled eggs, potatoes and thinly sliced sweet onions in a creamy mayonnaise. The mounds of fresh bread at each end of the table were already gone and Mme Bertrand went to cut more before bringing in a dish of

asparagus which she had bottled herself the previous
season. 'I'm afraid it is nothing like as good as when it is
fresh,' apologised M. Bertrand, dipping it in the vinaigrette,
and eating three helpings.

Next came a shallow tureen with a delicate aroma. 'What
is it?' the boys wanted to know.

'*C'est ris de veau,*' answered Madame proudly, '*avec olives
et petit champignons de Paris.*' She smiled as she watched them
taste it and we wondered how they would get on with
sweetbreads, but one trial mouthful of the succulent pieces
in their rich sauce was all that they needed. Neither were
conservative eaters; later that holiday they even tried roasted
sparrow which Philippe shot, and they caught fish in our
pond which they cooked on sticks over a camp fire. The
French family watched with approval as they ate their way
through plates of roast duck and *pommes forestières*. These
were potatoes sautéed with garlic and *cèpes* – the highly
prized toadstool found in the woods behind Bel-Air – and
sprinkled with fresh parsley. After salad we were offered
cheese. We had brought some English cheeses for them to
try. Grandpa enjoyed the mature cheddar but the rest of
the family clearly found it too strong, preferring the
Wensleydale and the Double Gloucester.

With the first few courses we had drunk a dry white wine
from Alsace but with the duck M. Bertrand produced a
dusty bottle very much like the one that we had so enjoyed
in November. Sure enough it was a vintage Cahors, and
had been bottled by Grandpa some twenty years before.
We sipped and savoured it with due reverence. For dessert
Madame presented a large home-made rhum baba which
she cut purposefully into ten slices, and while we were
eathing these I was disconcerted to see the substantial
Dundee cake which I had brought for them given the same
brisk treatment. I felt that I would have to wait until I knew
her a little better before I could explain the keeping qualities
of a Scottish fruit cake. I had not thought of rhum baba as
a French dish and I learned later that it was first introduced
into France in the middle of the eighteenth century by

Stanislas who, besides being the colourful king of Poland, was the father-in-law of Louis XV. It has remained popular ever since.

While Grandma poured the coffee Grandpa left the table to return with two bottles from which he offered us a choice of *eau-de-vie* made from plum or pear. This spirit was made on the farm by fermenting the fruit in wooden barrels. It was then distilled by the travelling still or *alambic* and it was so strong that I was glad that the glasses into which he carefully poured it were the smallest that I had ever seen. I noticed that neither of the women drank it and Mike finished most of mine. More to my taste was a delicious prune marinated in *eau-de-vie* which had been sweetened with sugar, and which had to be served into our still warm coffee cups.

This wonderful meal at last finished – it was by now past three-thirty – the children hunted for the Easter eggs which Madame had hidden. Philippe and his sister were intrigued with the English eggs filled with chocolate drops. I helped Madame and her mother to wash up while the men sat talking – not a situation encouraged in my family but when in Rome. . . . We were given a lift back up to our cold little ruin before it got too dark and loaded into the car with us were eggs, potatoes, onions, jars of jam and gherkins, wine and a lethal-looking scythe to tackle the waist-high brambles. It had been a marvellous Easter day in spite of the snow.

Mercifully the cold weather did not last and as the skies cleared the brilliance of the spring sunlight made us screw up our eyes each time we came out of doors. With the warmth came the wild flowers and the fields around Bel-Air were splashed with the sharp green and yellow of wild daffodils. White narcissi and vivid grape hyacinths glowed in the long grass. A cuckoo called confidently in the nearby wood, frogs in the now full-to-the-brim pond croaked in chorus night and morning and we could even hear the plaintive call of the peacocks in the garden of the château which, we were told, was just a few kilometres across the fields. We were simply too busy to go and look.

The wheat in the field at the back of the house (it was not to be maize this year) grew incredibly fast. The leaves on the ash trees began to uncurl. All this energy and activity exactly suited our mood and each time we came out of the house, on whichever side, we found ourselves saying 'Just look at that view!' It became a joke, but after London the sense of space was like a miracle. On cloudless days the sun was already hot enough to sit in without a coat. This was what we had come for. Our only problem was that we could not afford the time to enjoy just being lazy, there was so much that we wanted to do indoors.

The children from the farm often came up to help us. We seemed to be an attraction. With Veronique's assistance I cleared all the rubbish from the wide earth-floored corridor. In order to see we threw open the big oak door on the west side of the house and the strong breeze swung the thick cobwebs and the tattered shreds of linen bags of dried herbs, long since crumbled to dust. Veronique swept expertly with a besom, pressing the flat bristles into each corner like a rosy-cheeked Cinderella. Underneath yet more boxes and coils of rusty wire we found, set in the wall, the original, hand-hewn, granite sink and I determined to scrub it out thoroughly the next time we came.

As neither of the stoves in the main room worked we reluctantly moved them, chimney pipes and all, in order to clean the filthy wall behind them. There were only two lights in the house, both in the main room. One hung in the centre of the ceiling where, alas, the handsome original lamp had been and was no longer, and the other was a grimy bulb on the inside wall of the chimney which illuminated the fireplace. I cooked most meals on the open fire, burning up every single floor board from the great pile in the porch. I sat on Anaïs's special cooking chair with its cut down legs peering through the steam as I stirred my iron pot, my hair filling with wood smoke. My father's ancestors were gypsies and perhaps the contentment I felt

had something atavistic about it, even though I was indoors
– just. If I glanced up the wide chimney I could see the sky!

We scrubbed each wall in the main room and painted it
flat white. We mended the ceiling, replacing the rotten and
missing boards and we put down plastic sheets in the attic
until the *charpentier* could repair our roof. The children talked
a wonderful mixture of English and French. Strangely, and
without any prompting, our two attempted a sort of French
while Philippe practised his very good English. On being
asked which English book he was reading at school he
replied in his precise tones '*The Canteville Ghost* by Oscar
Wilde.'

'Blimey!' said our two and he learned another English
word.

Almost every day M. Bertrand would pass on his tractor
but with exquisite tact would turn to look away from the
house and only stop if we went out to greet him. Once he
did stop however, he was clearly eager to see what we were
doing. He told us how pleased he was to see Bel-Air cared
for once more. 'It looked so sad before,' he said. On the
second week of the holiday he warned us that the electric
fence would have to be switched on as he would be bringing
up some of his cows to their summer pasture.

All the next morning, helped by Grandma, he rumbled
slowly back and forth up to the house, the tractor in the
lowest possible gear, with two cows at a time tethered to
the trailer. Grandma walked behind with a stick, wearing
wellingtons, a flowered overall and a large straw hat, and
calling encouragement to the cows as they nodded their way
nervously up the track. The first to be untied was the largest
and oldest. She was to be 'Mother' and look after the
younger ones. Slowly and carefully M. Bertrand untied her
while we watched at a distance. It amused us to hear him
talking to her incessantly in soothing tones, praising her
sagesse and the beauty of the morning and the lushness of
the grass in the meadow that she would soon be able to
enjoy. Later he explained to us the very real danger from

her horns if she panicked – and also her value; she was worth almost seven hundred pounds. By midday nine young and beautiful *Blondes d'Aquitaine* stared at us over the fragile fence. Every few hours, led by Mother, they would trek past the house to drink at the pond and then, just as leisurely, file back up again to stand, like animals from a child's toy farmyard, in a straight line along the horizon.

The newly cemented floors in the two bedrooms were now solid enough to walk on. We took measurements. Each room was almost twelve feet square. We looked forward to moving into the bedrooms on our next trip in the summer. One had a magnificent view southwards down to the village and miles beyond. The other, once we had hacked away some of the straggling box trees, looked up the meadow to the cows and the distant woods. I decided that I would one day get rid of the box trees altogether. I hated their sour smell.

Our time was running out. We drew endless plans for studying back in London. We called again on the *charpentier* who confirmed that the roof would be done before July and that he would re-use as many of the old tiles as possible, mixing them carefully with the new. He showed us one of the new stop tiles which he intended to use underneath; these would, he said, prevent the upper tiles from sliding down as the old ones did whenever the French Air force jets made them jump with their supersonic bangs. 'They were not designed for that!' he smiled.

With a M. Albert, the plumber from the next village, we discussed the possibility of putting a lavatory and basin in the far pigsty. We did not feel we could face another holiday without that, but the bathroom proper would have to await more funds. He was another large, smiling man and very agreeable, but he explained that before he could begin we must contact M. René, our *maçon*, to install a septic tank or *fosse septique* first.

Consultation with M. René resulted in his arrival a few days later with a huge concrete *fosse* on the front of his bulldozer. There it hung until later that day when he came back with two of his workmen who immediately began to dig like beavers. M. René sped off in his van and the boys watched in amazement as the two small workmen went ever deeper throwing up great great clods of earth as they gradually disappeared. Not until they were down about ten feet did they stop and call for the ladder to get them out. Alas, it was on the van which had gone with M. René.

The boys searched the barn and dragged out the only ladder that they could find. It was completely worm-eaten and as we lowered it down we mimed that they must only tread on the outside edge of the few remaining rungs. Once the *fosse* was in situ M. René filled it with water. He told us that otherwise it would float up again if it rained hard.How much rain were they expecting we wondered?

No one would let us pay them. It was very strange. They said they were all friends of M. Bertrand and it could wait. The last days sped past and the morning when we had to leave for England arrived all too soon. We took a last look round. We covered the mattresses in plastic sheets and wondered about damp and mice. We loaded the van, locked the door and walked round once more to look at the view. How could we bear to go? High in a cloudless sky a lark poured out its effortless coloratura. The japonica was in flower, irises under the window were just beginning to unwrap their white, scented petals and everywhere there were swellings of buds that I would not see unfold.

We climbed into what seemed an incredibly spacious van, took a last look at our beloved house and drove very slowly down the track to the farm. There on the table, lined up for us to take, were a carton of eggs, a jar of prunes in *eau-de-vie*, bottled greengages and pears, bunches of onions and the wicker-covered *bonbonne* of wine. We stowed them all in the van and went in for a last cup of coffee. Grandma had made a tin of *gauffres*, a rolled-up crisp wafer biscuit, for the boys to eat on the journey. They all hoped the dreaded channel would not be too rough.

As we climbed at last into the van Grandpa came to say

goodbye clutching what looked like a bottle of mineral water. We guessed from the grin on his face that it was in fact his precious *eau-de-vie*. 'I haven't filled it to the top,' he said. 'That way it will look more like water for the journey. If they ask you can always say it's from Lourdes.'

'And if they taste it?'

'Say it's a miracle!' he shouted throwing up his arms in delight. They all stood waving until we turned the corner and set our faces northwards.

5

Mike, who was then still lecturing at Goldsmiths' college, had eight weeks' summer vacation and I simply drew a line through the whole of Matthew's school holidays and accepted no bookings. For the first time in my life I did not want to work, I just longed to get to France. Our other son Adam was, alas, off on yet another tour. Many friends, eager to see what we had bought, announced their intentions of coming to stay. In vain we described its near derelict state; the one, cold, outside tap, the distinct possibility of our lavatory in the pigsty not being finished; but it was impossible to dissuade them and I suppose that we did not try very hard. One of the many joys of Bel-Air has turned out to be the sharing of it with friends.

We drove down as usual without an inch to spare. Matthew and the indomitable Durrell hung onto a secondhand fridge insecurely wedged between more beds, a chest of drawers, and boxes of those things which were, at that time, twice as expensive or unobtainable in France; tissues and toilet rolls, orange juice and butter, tea and marmite. It is interesting that now prices are almost comparable except for cheese which I still find inexplicably more expensive in France, milk being much the same price.

There were no clouds and a brilliant full moon rose to light our way. We sped through the silent villages, their traffic lights set at winking amber, and as the sun came up and slowly climbed round to face us we rejoiced to be going south. Before midday we drove past the château and round the last bend to our village. We turned by the church and as we swung into the drive up to the farm Mme Bertrand waved to us from the kitchen garden where she was weeding. The courtyard was full of flowers, boxes of tumbling geraniums beneath the veranda windows and a lemon tree covered in fruit in a tub by the door. M. Bertrand climbed down from his tractor with a broad smile and, across the yard, wiping his hands on his trousers, came Grandpa to greet us, his dogs at his heels.

'Was the roof finished? Did the lavatory work?' M. Bertrand would not say but his face gave us the answer. Grandma took me by the hand and led me through the farm yard, past her small house, past the silo and the chicken barn and, at the far end, she pointed across the fields and up beyond. I had not realised that Bel-Air was so clearly visible from there. I could see the roof, an attractive mottling of old and new tiles. She smiled at my relief.

We drove up the now dry and firm track to the house, turned in and stopped before our porch. On the low walls were yellow plastic washing-up bowls filled with petunias and geraniums. Pots of huge scarlet begonias draped the top of the well. The shutters had been opened and the sun streamed in on the long table laden with vegetables, eggs and wine. There were fresh flowers, marguerites and asters, and even a little bunch of parsley tied with cotton. We could not have felt more welcome.

The roof looked even better close to. The rotten cross beam on the porch had been replaced with an old but solid telegraph pole and all the jointing was with stout wooden pegs. I was so pleased that the *charpentier* had conserved *le style*. It had had to be repaired but its very dereliction had held such charm for me. The two bedrooms were now habitable, and after unloading, what had seemed in the van a great deal of furniture was soon lost. The following day we gave the bedroom walls a coat of flat white but further work indoors was impossible.

We needed the sun. That was why we were there. We decided to attack the great pile of old broken tiles that the *charpentier* had simply left on the grass on the south-facing side of the house. Hammering them into small pieces was a satisfying task. In bucket loads I carried them to help fill in the holes in the track and, even in a bikini, it was hot work. Grandpa came up on a tour of inspection.

'*Oui. Elle est vaillante,*' he nodded his approval. '*Elle travaille bien,*' he said to Mike. I felt he might give me a lump of sugar at any moment.

In the smallest pigsty, the floor and walls newly cemented, sat our brand new lavatory and a hand basin with a single cold tap. These simplest of conveniences gave us enormous pleasure. Indeed the joy of a lavatory from which one could contemplate several miles of gently sloping meadow was to later inspire our friend the poet to many a verse. The field at the back of the house had already been harvested and was covered with straw. All day long M. Bertrand worked on the baler. A somewhat ancient machine with a leg at the back like a manic grasshopper, it would periodically stop its clacking when it either ran out of twine or broke down altogether. Then M. Bertrand would come up to Bel-Air for a cold drink, the sweat trickling down from under the brim of his hat. The straw dust sticking to his hands and arms he would drain two or three long glasses. '*Ah, ça fait plaisir!*' he would sigh and then off he would go and the baler would clatter down the next row of straw.

At last it was finished and *le grand champ*, as he always called it, was scattered with square bales.

'*Eh Alors,*' he said, '*demain on ramasse la paille.*' Tomorrow we harvest the straw. (*Ramasser,* to harvest, was one of the first verbs I learned.)

'How many of you?' we asked.

'*Toute la famille,*' he replied, '*et . . . quelques amis aussi, sans doute.*'

'May we help?' we asked.

He smiled. '*Bien sûr! Mais . . . vous êtes en vacance.*'

On holiday? We laughed. Breaking up tiles, painting, plastering? *Le grand champ* was blurred in heat haze and looked inviting.

At eight-thirty next morning the sky was like that of a travel brochure and the air sweet and cool. As instructed we all wore gloves. Already in the field were M. Bertrand and the rest of the family, Grandma and Grandpa both wearing large brimmed straw hats and we were introduced to a handsome moustachioed newcomer who, it turned out, was the Mayor. Pitchfork in hand, M. Bertrand stood on the trailer to which was attached a mechanical arm. He showed us how to drop the bales of straw so that they would be propelled upward where he would catch them on his fork and arrange them neatly. It seemed simple and we began to work. Grandpa watched us for a few minutes then came towards us shaking his head. '*Pas si vite!*' Not so fast, he shouted. 'For one hour perhaps but for all day – no!'

As the sun rose higher we understood. It was necessary to establish a rhythm. The men, scorning the mechanical arm, hurled the bales up on their pitchforks, M. Bertrand worked like a demon on an ever-mounting pile. The cart full, Mike was eager to drive the tractor. He was allowed to fetch the empty trailer, but once M. Bertrand had seen that he was competent he soon entrusted him with a full load. The separate braking system on a tractor is very similar to that on a tank, Mike explained to the boys. It was obvious to me that he was in his element.

There was no mid-morning coffee break; we worked solidly for four hours. Now we really appreciated Grandpa's admonition. The dogs chased the mice which ran through the stubble each time we started on a new pile of bales and, just before twelve, Mme Bertrand disappeared to prepare the meal. The bell for midday sounded from the church and half an hour later we stopped, very tired but filled with fresh air and sunshine.

'*Alors!*' called M. Bertrand from the top of the loaded cart, '*Allez manger!*' We demurred. '*Mai si!*' he shouted. Grandpa stuck his fork in halfway down the load enabling him to jump down. '*Ceux qui travaillent doivent manger. C'est normal,*' he continued. The boys did not need telling twice, they were already climbing up on the tractor to ride back to the farm.

What exquisite pleasure to peel off sweat-filled gloves and wash my hands under the tap in the cool kitchen. After an aperitif we drained glass after glass of water. The meal began with slices of melon and home-cured ham. Then we ate cucumber and onion salad. A dish of white beans in tomato sauce which delighted the boys and was pronounced much better than Heinz, was followed by grilled steaks and a green salad. We were ravenous. Peaches picked the previous day and pears, the first from the orchard, completed the meal. It was not until after two-thirty that we left the table and, rested and refreshed, went back to finish off *le grand champ*.

So began our tradition of helping the family whenever we could. It gave us a much greater insight into the life of the people amongst whom we were living and an awareness of the crops and the weather. A heavy fall of rain which we might have considered merely a nuisance became instead just what was needed to swell the plums or the maize and we learned so much; M. Bertrand was a wonderfully patient teacher – he never appeared to tire of our endless questions.

Our first visitors being due any day we decided that we must buy a cooker. Obviously it would have to be the cheapest one we could find and so we made our first real exploration of our nearest town of Monflanquin. Until then our forays into town had been swift, for fresh milk or meat, the only two things *not* sold in our village shop. This afternoon we took time to walk up the steep street – each small house decked with begonias, geraniums or strings of morning glories – through the arcaded square and past the originally fortified church to the highest point, the Cap del Pech, from where there is a wonderful panoramic view. It was a clear day and some twelve kilometres distant the Château of Biron lay like a great liner on the blue horizon.

How safe the original Monflanquinois must have felt. Those 'new-towners' of 1252, encouraged to come and build a house in this *Bastide* – one of a chain of such fortified towns built across south-west France. Monflanquin was the creation of Alphonse de Poitiers, Comte de Toulouse and brother of the King. He planted his staff, complete with escutcheon, at the centre point of the proposed town and the streets were then marked out at right angles in furrows. Until the houses were built the whole place must have looked like a great market garden.

Each inhabitant, who had a year and a day in which to complete his house, was allocated also two pieces of land for cultivation outside the walls. Under the protection of the Seigneur, Monflanquin had its own charter devised to cover every conceivable problem which might arise in such a close-living community, from damage or theft of crops or livestock, the settling of dispute by fines – five sols for a blow by fist or foot, twenty sols if blood were drawn, sixty if a weapon were used – to the obligatory running naked through the town of those caught *en flagrant délit* and unwilling or unable to pay 100 sols.

Before Monflanquin was fifty years old the King and his brother were both dead and Aquitaine was handed back to the English. One can only wonder what the then six hundred and twenty inhabitants thought as Edward I, King of England, and his procession wound their way up the hillside to make solemn entry through the gates in 1289.

We dragged ourselves from the mesmeric view and went in search of our cooker which, with its accompanying bottle of Calor gas, was delivered the following day.

'Where shall I put it?' enquired the sleek-haired shop keeper. Just inside the door seemed at that moment the easiest place. It looked incongruously new and rectangular against the sloping wall. *'Formidable!'* he exclaimed when he tested it. I have used many words to describe it since that day; *formidable* is not one of them.

Our visitors arrived. Arno Rabinowitz, his wife and son, all confirmed Francophiles, seemed delighted with Bel-Air, les Bertrands and the region. Arno soon endeared himself to Grandpa by proving to be a dab hand at *belote*, the local card game; their fluent French (they had lived in Lille for two years) put my attempts to shame and I resolved then and there to find somewhere in London to study seriously on my return.

Arno, then the chief psychologist for south London schools, as his own therapy chose to clear an area outside the porch where we always ate breakfast, it being the first corner touched by the early morning sun. He hacked out the tough grass and weeds and small seedling ash trees, laid sand and gravel, and raked it smooth until we had a small passable terrace on which to put their camping table and an assortment of chairs. There we would daily break our fast and sit in the sun until it eventually turned the corner and we, picking up our chairs, would follow it.

We discovered the joy of having a garden on four sides where one could always follow the sun or avoid the wind. In my imagination four different gardens were planned, the southfacing one tropical with bananas and poinsettias, but alas, even after twelve summers I am far from achieving it. Dealing with a garden which is left to the whims of nature for months at a time demands a certain resignation. Progress is snail-like. But the satisfaction of disinterring it from weeds, and rampant virginia creeper, and the sudden abundant flourishing of forgotten plantings are, I have decided, my kind of gardening.

Each holiday I rush round on arriving to see just what has survived. The occasional disappointment over a shrub that did not make it is compensated for by the incredible growth of clematis and passion flowers. My hardy house leeks, from an original clump which Anaïs, my predecessor, had planted on the west-facing roof of the end pigsty, have been transplanted into borders and proliferate and, when conditions are exactly right, flower exotically. One root of a tall yellow daisy brought from my London garden where, to get enough sunlight it would always lean and twist its rough stems, is at Bel-Air part of a thick straight hedge of flowers, and I have a row of Chinese lanterns that nothing can destroy. A hydrangea panniculata which, after a disastrous beginning in the limey garden soil into which I thoughtlessly put it, has this year, from the safety of a pot, rewarded my belated care with sixteen huge blooms. It must rely for watering on the rain which runs off the roof. And my pomegranate which I thought had not survived the bitter winters of '85 and '86 is this summer shooting madly again. Gardens are full of miracles.

The days flew by and as the Rabinowitzes made their farewells we awaited the arrival of our next guests, Barry Foster, the actor, his wife and three children who were expected in mid-August. Judith and the children were to stay on when Barry had to return for the filming of 'The Three Hostages'. On August 14, early in the evening, Mme Bertrand came up to tell us that 'Monsieur Fostaire' had just telephoned. The radiator in his BMW had burst and he was stranded near Bergerac. The following day was the Feast of the Assumption and everything, including garages, would be shut.

We borrowed a towrope and set off and some forty minutes later we were hugging, laughing and kissing one another. The rope secured we began the return to Bel-Air. What we did not know was that our braking lights on the camper only worked when the brakes were fully applied and Barry told us later of the constant, unexpected looming of our high white rear, each time dangerously close. Crossing our threshold at last, tired and travel-worn, he looked round. 'OK,' he said, 'this'll do. I reckon I can lock off here.' We opened a bottle and drank a toast.

Les Bertrands, who had seen 'Le Fostaire' on French television, were delighted to meet him in the flesh. The girls, Joanna and Miranda, mere teenagers then, explored everywhere with shrieks of delight and Jason, who was the same age as Matthew and Philippe, just disappeared with them. We sampled all the local markets. There seemed to be one somewhere almost every day of the week. We would stagger home with trays of melons and peaches, nectarines and apricots, bunches of fresh basil, baskets of wild strawberries and feasts of mussels, oysters and fresh sardines. Mme Bertrand would bring us french beans and courgettes and eggs with dark yellow yolks. We grilled the local sausages and sweet pork cutlets sprinkled with herbs on a wood fire outside and we sampled each local wine. The *Cave Coopérative* at Monflanquin was in the process of being enlarged and improved and in 1985 won a gold medal in Paris.

One morning the girls, having been warned to tread carefully, decided to explore the attic which ran the whole length of the house. They were intrigued by a yellowing, footless stocking which hung from the ceiling in the main room downstairs. As dust from between the floorboards fell on us below we could hear them laughing and Joanna suddenly reappeared. 'Watch this, it's so simple,' she said. She put a basket on the floor, shouted 'Right!' and Miranda filled it by dropping down through the stocking dried corn cobs from a pile they had found. They discovered two old wine racks, crudely made, a wooden rake, a beautiful hay fork, two very primitive tools for teasing out sheep's wool and a strange wooden object, a cross between a cradle and a sledge, but clearly neither, for which none of us could imagine a purpose. We would have to ask Grandma. By now we were all up in the attic.

There were more boxes full of cobwebbed bottles. Some were the dark blue, flat perfume bottles which had held 'Evening in Paris' by Bourjois. We wondered if it had been the son Alaïs who had saved up to buy his mother perfume for her birthday perhaps or had these sad, dusty bottles been presents from her husband Justin before he died. I now knew that Anaïs had woken to find him dead beside her from a heart attack sometime in 1918. There were bottles which had contained Castor Oil, Quinine, Seidlitz powders and Balm and several which were marked Caiffa. This was not to be found in any dictionary and was clearly another question for Grandma. We washed the more attractive bottles and put them on shelves on the porch.

At the far end of the attic, behind all the tools and boxes, was a sideboard, even older and larger than the one downstairs. It had a key in the door but was not locked. It was stuffed with old newspapers, calendars, parish magazines and in one corner was an oval cardboard hat box with a lid. We sat on the floor looking at the mouldering school books, the letters chewed by generations of mice and the folded documents that it contained. These would have to wait until we had both the time and the French to decipher them. In the meantime the sideboard, if we could get it there, would be very useful downstairs. We had an hilarious hour inching the truly massive object cross the uneven, rotting floorboards to the opposite end of the attic and down the crumbling staircase. We scrubbed it with bleach and left it in the sun to dry a handsome colour. Later we saw similar sideboards in an antique shop for several hundred pounds.

As it was our wedding anniversary and also Barry's birthday in a few days, we planned a celebration. It was an opportunity to return a little of the hospitality of the Bertrands and we also invited the builder M. René, his wife and grandson, and some English friends who were holidaying not far away. We planned a menu. We could not hope to compete with Mme Bertrand, or Claudette as she now was, but we felt that we must, at least, give them sufficient to eat and prove that, contrary to popular belief, the English *can* cook.

In the midst of our planning the weather broke. Our visions of a warm, moonlit soirée under the stars with, perhaps, candles in jars hung from the ash tree faded, as the Westerlies lashed in from the Atlantic bearing dark, rain-filled clouds. The thermometer dropped and dropped. It seemed incredible that only a few days before it had been 85 degrees in the shade. We learned about the unpredictability of August in Aquitaine. It was indeed the land of the waters.

It rained and rained. 'Les Fostaires' had two pairs of wellingtons between them. They had, like us, expected unlimited sunshine. The water ran in torrents down the fields and became trapped in front of the house where it joined the cascade from the roof. Arno's terrace it now appeared had not been such a good idea. It was covering the channel to carry away the water. Barry, ankle deep in the muddy river which now threatened to flood the house, wielded a great hoe to cut trenches to divert the flow. 'I'm afraid Rabinowitz's terrace is now Foster's battle field,' he yelled over the drumming downpour. We realised that something would have to be done about a gutter and a drain.

The house saved from flooding, we returned to our plans. Unknown to Mike or Barry we baked a large fruit cake and went into the nearest town for decorations and candles. It was so damp and cold that we had to light a fire and inevitably that meant many hours enjoying sitting round it. Time passed under the illusion that something was happening as we were mesmerised by its ever-changing form. What could we give them to eat? With the weather so wintry our thoughts turned to hot dishes, but we decided to begin the meal with a great salad Niçoise. It would at least be familiar. Then as a novelty for the French guests we planned to follow it with a deluxe version of Shepherd's pie with garlic and mushrooms and for the children we made jellies filled with fruit and finally we would serve the cake. It was a somewhat arbitrary menu but once we had decided we felt a great sense of relief and got on with it. We would be twenty in all so there was much to do and a great deal of improvising with pots and pans. At least we now had a refrigerator in which to chill the white wine and the champagne.

At eight o'clock, bearing flowers and little gifts, they

arrived. Simone, M. René's wife brought two china angels, Claudette, a pair of decorative candles. One pair of English friends gave us a copper ladle and another pair, as a comment on the weather, brought a stone hot water bottle. The party was a great success. Our French guests looked relieved when we served the salad. They had obviously been apprehensive and still looked sideways at the three large Shepherd's pies keeping hot on trivets at the edge of the fire.

'*C'est le repas du berger,*' we encouraged.

'*Ça sent bon,*' said M. Bertrand, or Raymond, as we now called him, '*Mais* . . . he hesitated. Claudette was unabashed.

'*Qu'est ce qu'il y a dedans*?' What's in it? she demanded.

The list of ingredients, including garlic and parsley, reassured them sufficiently to take minute helpings to begin with, followed by larger platefuls, until the Shepherd's pies were no more. Mutual relief!

The biggest surprise was the reaction to the jelly. True it was made with orange juice and stuffed with fresh fruit but the adults enjoyed it as much as the children. Raymond had two helpings and Claudette asked if we would bring jellies with us on our next trip, and so they went on the list. There is always a list for *la prochaine fois* – the next time.

The lights were turned out, all two of them, and our French guests actually chorused '*oh la la!*' as Joanna brought in the cake with candles blazing. We sang 'Happy Birthday' and 'Happy Anniversary' and every song we could remember in English and in French. Judith and I, who had first met in the chorus of 'Kismet' – light years ago – attempted duets and Raymond tried to teach us local songs in patois. This was difficult as, although he was the only one with the courage to sing solo, he could not hold a tune. With more enthusiasm than accuracy he changed key before the end of each verse. But he loved to listen, clapping like a demon at the end and immediately demanding another. He was a great guest, truly the life and soul of the party.

Parties were, in fact, one of his specialities as we were to discover later.

As it always does, the weather improved and the sun was twice as strong as it ever is in London. We took Barry to Cahors, home of the wonderful dark wine, to catch the Paris train. 'Some of us have to work,' he said wryly looking up at the cloudless blue. Judith and the children stayed on and as the tobacco was to be harvested we asked if we might help. The dark green rows resembled giant, flowerless gladioli but the leaves were broader and more fragile. Grandpa showed Mike how to fell each plant with a small axe so that they all lay in the same direction. We lifted them one at a time, balancing each heavy sheaf across one arm like a large bouquet, and were careful not to damage the leaves as we laid them along the edge of the nearby trailer. When the floor of the trailer was covered we walked behind it down to the tobacco-drying shed or *séchoir*.

A large barn, some eight metres high, it had a raised platform near the door against which the trailer of tobacco was carefully positioned. The reason soon became clear. Standing on the platform we were able, without effort, to reach the sheaves. Grandma handed us all a stout, four-pronged hook. 'Watch,' she said. Above the platform, at head-height, there was a line strung across the shed with a row of short metal rods suspended from it. She fixed the pronged hook to the bottom of the rod, lifted a sheaf of tobacco by its thick stem and, pushing the hook through it, suspended it upside down. When all four hooks were full we detached the whole thing and carried it across the shed to where Raymond waited with a rickety pulley. He hoisted them up gradually until there were five sets of four sheaves, one below the other. Now the reason for the great height of the shed was clear. As it began to fill with its canopy of dense green foliage it was like some exotic jungle or a set for a commercial for coconut bars.

Again we sang. Raymond started it. '*Chantez Philippe, chantez Véronique*,' he shouted. France had just won the

Eurovision song contest with a surprisingly reasonable song about a child and a bird and I remember Véronique's sweet small voice in that cool leafy interior while the sun blazed outside. Pushing the hooks through the tough stems made my fingers ache and, as I so often do, I watched Grandma and marvelled at the strength in her apparently frail body. Raymond grumbled about the low prices the dealers would give for the leaves when they were dry and taken to market.

'How long will it take for them to dry?' we asked.

He shrugged. *'Ça dépend du temps.'* It depends on the weather. The farmer's universal cry, but we had already begun to appreciate that in this corner of France it was unpredictable.

And, once again, we all ate round the farm table. So many meals we have enjoyed there. Claudette seems to think nothing of working three or four hours in the fields and then preparing six or seven courses for a dozen or more. Grandma scurries about to help her and everything is grown or prepared on the farm. And the melons! This summer was our first real gorging on the local, small, Charentais melon. Round, striped green and yellow with perfumed apricot flesh, once the season has started there is an abundance. That year was particularly good and our friends kept us supplied.

'They must be eaten,' Claudette would insist, bringing us another basketfull. We ate them at every meal — especially breakfast. What joy to find a *gourmandise* that did not fatten!

'Les Fostaires' left eventually for England and we began to realise that we too would soon have to close up our house in the sun and go back to London. The weather was still perfect. The evenings were shorter but it was still warm enough to eat outside and wait in the silent darkness for the first stars to appear. Sometimes a satellite would trace a path across the universe. How would we adjust?

The list of things for Easter '78 grew ever longer. In exchange for the original furniture in Bel-Air we had agreed to bring out, the next time we came, anoraks and sweaters for the children and a Black and Decker drill, all much cheaper in England. We planned and measured. Where could we put a bathroom when we could afford it? What about the kitchen? Washing up in a plastic bowl on a sloping camping table had lost its appeal. Should we make the small south-facing room off the main room into a kitchen? We could not decide.

'Think about it,' said M. Albert, the plumber, 'and let me know when you come again next Easter.' At that moment Easter seemed an awfully long way ahead.

We closed the rickety shutters, just another thing that needed repairing, and we locked the door. Bumping down the track for the last time we hung out of the windows to get our last glimpse. Strange, we never did this when we left London.

'*À la prochaine fois!*'

6

Easter the following year was early and cold but there
was no snow. We spent many hours collecting firewood,
there being, alas, no floorboards left to burn. Now we
understood the neat woodstacks adjoining local houses.
Fortunately Matthew and Durrell enjoyed dragging dead
trees from the wood and sawing them up. They whittled
sticks to make individual, decorated toasting forks. These
normally centrally-heated youths were endlessly fascinated
by the great open fire.

The house was full of vases of wild daffodils and Grandma
had planted the yellow washing-up bowls with great purple
pansies. We cleared the straggly hazel hedge which
obscured our view up the meadow from the front door and
I began to dream about a terrace on the opposite, south-
facing side of the house. This became my special project
but, due to sheer incompetence, it took me several years
to finish. The preliminary clearing of the ground was made
difficult by stubborn lengths of old chicken wire embedded
in the soil. It seemed probable that this was where Anaïs's
poultry had once scratched and squawked and each time
I thought that I had removed the last tenacious piece,

another buried end taunted me. The clean sweet air and the view which greeted me each time I straightened up kept me going.

The debate continued about where to put the kitchen. Now that the other two bedrooms were habitable, should we make use of the small, low-ceilinged room which adjoined the main room? We might, perhaps, knock through a hatch, or even remove the upper half of the wall completely. We simply could not decide and eventually we did nothing. Just inside the front door where, after scraping the green lichen from the wall to paint it, we had first installed the cooker, became the kitchen's permanent place. The ever-open door provided an extractor and all we needed now was a worktop and a sink.

We consulted M. Albert the plumber. Yes, it was possible. The long runaway out to the septic tank which we had thought might be a problem did not seem to bother him. As he pointed out, the floor of the corridor was still earth. We chose a large, plain white china sink and M. Albert recommended a carpenter to build us a pine surround. A kitchen corner began to take shape. I felt that in a holiday home where all were encouraged to help, a separate kitchen was not a good idea and I had noticed that most of the simple local homes into which we had been invited were so arranged.

M. Brut, the local *menuisier* or carpenter was clearly impressed by Mike's rough designs for two wall cupboards and a worktop. *'Pardi!'* he exclaimed, switching off his saw and brushing the mountain of wood-shavings off his desk to clear a space. *Pardi*, an archaic corruption of *Par Dieu* – By God – is one of M. Brut's favourite expressions. He also undertook to replace those of our shutters which were beyond repair and when we returned that summer we were delighted to find all the work completed.

What joy to wash up under hot running water! One of the bonuses of having lived so primitively in the beginning was the enormous pleasure at each improvement. The pine cupboards and surround were, like M. Brut himself, handsome and solid, the long ornamental hinges were very French and, most important of all, the cupboards were totally mouse-proof. *Et voilà*, a kitchen corner. In fact most of the preparation of food is done out-of-doors, sitting on the porch or in the sun. The only thing we had not bargained for was M. Albert's unfortunate positioning of the water heater. With about eighteen feet of wall to choose from he had fixed it right beside the original hand-hewn granite sink that we had uncovered. Its handsome edging stones were now partially obscured by a modern multipoint that would clearly at some time have to be re-sited, but I consoled myself with hot soap suds.

As it was now not needed for a kitchen we thought again about the small, low-ceilinged room which faced south. One hot morning after breakfast we stood looking up at the badly worm-eaten false ceiling of tongued and grooved pine. Were the worms still active? Was it worth treating? We wandered out into the wide earth corridor behind it and looked up. There, at least two feet higher, were the original oak boards and massive beams which must surely run across above the worm-eaten pine. We looked at each other and, as with most jobs that we have done ourselves at Bel-Air, the decision was mutual and, once voiced, instantly begun.

Down came the dusty slats. Leaves, cobwebs, mouse and bat droppings filled our hair and eyes but, as we had hoped, we uncovered the original boards and beams. Gleefully we worked all morning, carrying out the worm-eaten slats to form a welcome stack of firewood. The plaster on the exterior wall of the room was loose and crumbled away as we brushed against it. We realised that it was simply a crude earth mixture that would have to come down at some time and we were in a demolition mood. We had a ten minute break for food (how un-French!) and then began, gently at first, to knock away the earth.

What excitement! The floor was soon covered with dry clods and through the choking dust we could see the wonderful stones emerging. They were far too handsome to be plastered. We could have them cleaned and leave this wall in *pierres apparentes* as it is called. The joins between the stones we would fill with a light-coloured cement and leave the stones proud. Once begun it was compulsive. All afternoon we worked, dragging the rickety ladder from the barn to supplement our small stepladder. There were far more urgent tasks waiting but we did not care. When the wall was almost finished we heard Raymond chugging up the track. He switched off the engine and wiping the sweat from his eyes climbed down from the tractor. *'Viens, viens!'* we shouted. His face made me laugh aloud. His mouth dropped open as he gazed alternately up at the ceiling and down to the chaos on the floor.

'Mais . . . qu'est-ce que vous faites?' he cried, his dark eyes round as marbles. It was plain that he considered us quite mad but did not like to say as much.

By now we had seen that the pattern of the stones continued on the other side of the newer, thin wall which divided this room from the bottom of the staircase, and would extend to the original window with the iron-studded door above it. We explained that we thought of moving the interior wall back to include this window with its hand-cut stone opening and transom. Raymond nodded gravely. *'Oui, la fenêtre est jolie. Elle est tellement ancienne.'* He looked suddenly relieved. Perhaps these English were not entirely crazy.

Needing something with which to clear the floor I looked up the word for wheelbarrow. I followed him to the barn where he unearthed for me the oldest wooden barrow I'd ever seen. He smiled as I tugged at the handles. *'C'était avec celle-là que Anaïs faisait ses commissions au village'*, he said. It takes me fifteen minutes at least to walk to the village shop and it is downhill all the way. I imagined having to pull this barrow, loaded with shopping, back up the bumpy track and I was once more humbled by the hard life of my predecessor. I longed to know more about her.

I felt her presence strongly, there were so many of her things still in the house. In the drawer of the sideboard which she had polished I found her rusted needles in a wooden case, dusty spools of thread, worn wooden spindles and dozens of rolled up strips of material torn from shirt tails. The boys, imagining they might contain treasures, unrolled a few but they were simply scraps for patching, a sign of her poverty and thrift.

As she had promised, Grandma had brought me the photograph. Anaïs must have been in her early thirties when it was taken. A strong, handsome woman in a dark dress and white cap she stands protectively behind a sturdy boy of about twelve years, who is holding a hoop. Was this taken before he caught polio or was it just a thoughtlessly cruel photographer's prop? They look confidently enough into the camera, unaware of the tragedies to befall them; a sad contrast with Raymond's description of the last days of a frail and bed-ridden, ninety-two-year-old Anaïs and her semi-paralysed, reclusive and elderly son. I had the photograph copied and now they hang beside the sideboard where I feel they belong. After all, Anaïs lived at Bel-Air for over fifty years.

As I now turned on my tap for unlimited hot water I thought about the tiny water compartment in Anaïs's stove that we had removed. I imagined her chopping the sticks to light it, as my own Mother had done on those far off Monday wash-days of my childhood. (I remembered too the mad scrambles to unpeg everything when the first shout of 'raining' was heard across the back gardens.) Here the washing dries so quickly. I stretched a line from Raymond's barn to the ash tree and nothing smells sweeter than clothes dried in a hot sun and a strong wind blowing across flower-filled meadows.

Of course it does rain here. On such a day when I had been finally driven from the garden by heavy squalls at twenty minute intervals, I remembered Anaïs's battered cardboard hat box which we had found in the attic. It seemed a good moment to take a closer look at the contents. My French was improving for I had found a course at Morley College and had gone right back to the beginning with a very young and equally fierce Mme Rousseau whose teaching methods were, to me, a revelation. Simple but amusing texts, the dramatising of scenes transposed from one tense to another, extracts from current magazines and newspapers, poems by Prévert and songs by Brassens, and the severity with which she corrected us in the language laboratory kept me enthralled. It is due to her hard work and the later inspiration of Madeleine Enright and Georgette Butler, also at Morley, that I have at last progressed to the joys of Flaubert and Victor Hugo, Molière and Anouilh. But I still make idiotic mistakes and would dearly love to be truly bilingual.

Almost the first thing I opened, after I had dusted everything in the box and shaken out the mouse droppings and dehydrated spiders, was Anaïs's school reader. A 'new' edition of *La Petite Jeanne* published in 1876 with her maiden name 'Anaïs Mauriac' laboriously written inside. Although tattered it had not actually been chewed by mice as had so many of the letters beneath it. Blessed and approved by no less than a cardinal, an archbishop and three bishops it is, as one might expect, the most moral of tales and yet has a simplicity that reminded me of Flaubert's *Un Coeur Simple*. It is Jeanne's story from early childhood to the grave and the four sections into which it is divided, childhood, in service, wife and mother, and widowhood, prophetically chart the life of Anaïs herself and, I imagine a great many other girls of that time.

It is illustrated with charming engravings, and Anaïis had clearly read and re-read it, absorbing its moral and practical precepts. She had glued a strip of flannelette down the spine to hold the fragile, much-fingered pages together. As I began to read I was amazed by the scores of household hints woven into the story and the tips on animal husbandry and crop rotation. There is a passage describing the astonishment of the village women at the way Jeanne looks after her children; *'Comme s'ils étaient les enfants de bourgeois!'* Because they are peasants should they be dirty? is her reply, explaining that each night she folds their clothes before laying them in a chest and at mealtimes ties a napkin round their necks. Growing flax she spins cloth which, in hard times, keeps her out of debt. On the last page of the wife and mother section, are the words with which the Curé tries to comfort Jeanne on the sudden death of her husband. '*Ma fille, comme c'est la volonté de Dieu que vous soyez séparés, il faut bien s'y soumettre.*' There was something written in the margin in faint pencil and I moved to the window to try to decipher it. I felt her presence very close at that moment as I read what Anaïs, a widow at forty-seven, had written in her school reader which had clearly served her for so many years. '*Mort de Justin*' was the simple statement.

The following week M. René, the *maçon*, came up to advise us on enlarging the small room with its bare stone wall and newly exposed beams. Yes, it was certainly possible to move the modern, interior wall, in fact he would recommend it as it was none too stable. He became quite excited at the thought of including the ancient window and suggested that we might also move the other wall back some three feet into the corridor, thus making a splendid main bedroom. The narrow space remaining beyond the window was now taken up solely by the crumbling staircase which would, in any case, need replacing. But did we really need a staircase? With three large bedrooms on the ground floor and the possibility, at some stage, of converting the *chai*, the attic would seem to be of more use as storage space. In that case a loft ladder would do and the staircase area could be used for a bathroom.

A bathroom. What a wonderful thought. The pleasures of a long, hot soak after hours of back-breaking work came nearer when we discussed our plans with M. Albert. He also suggested that while he and M. René were at it, they might build an indoor lavatory in the space at the far end of the corridor. Two lavatories. Heaven. But we still prefer the one with the view, as does our first friend to arrive that summer, the poet, Anthony Saville White. A firm friend since student days, king of puns, word-spinner and enthusiast, he was moved to write a series of verses while gazing, seated, admiring the sweep of meadow up to the woods beyond.

This, his first visit, was made on a giant motorbike. He picked the only wet night that summer and sodden and exhausted, having ridden all the way from Northumberland, could not find our track in the dark. About midnight, utterly lost, he finally arrived *chez Bertrand* and gallant Raymond got out of bed to bring him up to us. Since that first visit he has returned in a variety of ways; by car with his family, and once, unexpectedly, by air, as the only non-devout passenger on a pilgrimage to Lourdes. That night, since we were out, he rolled himself in a blanket to doze in a deck chair on the porch from which, on our return, he rose spectre-like in the moonlight, declaiming something or other – I forget what. On another occasion, in a Herculean effort, with Nancy his indefatigable wife, he came by bicycle. We now await his arrival by balloon.

This first visit, after his wet arrival, coincided with a spell of spectacular weather. The sun shone all day, every day, in a cloudless heaven but we were refreshed by a gentle breeze from the North. '*Le grand beau temps est arrivé,*' pronounced Grandpa when he trudged up, staff in hand, to check the fences. Day after day it continued and how we revelled in it. The air was heavy with the drone of insects, butterflies with pleated wings flitted through the poppies and blue chicory that lined the track, and lizards, immobile but for the pulse under their throat, lay on the hot stones. There was a great sense of peace and completeness.

Mike, who tans in ten minutes' sun and was dubbed by Tony 'old teak face', sat drawing the field of maize. It whispered and crackled in the heat shimmer and grew so fast that eventually Mike had to sit on the top of the stepladder to finish the drawing. Matthew asked if he might pick some sweetcorn to eat. Raymond looked horrified. '*Bien sûr,*' he cried, '*mais, c'est pour les bêtes!*' We did cook some and it was quite good but we could never persuade Raymond to try it. As far as he was concerned it was on a par with another English abomination, mint sauce.

This holiday we had brought with us a large leg of English lamb. We knew that it would be a treat for *les Bertrand*, being firstly an animal that they did *not* rear and secondly, at that time, more than twice as expensive in France. We planned to invite the whole family for Sunday lunch to give Claudette a free day and to return just a little of their incredible hospitality. With my limited kitchen facilities I planned a menu, aware of the need for quantity, as well as tastes, to intrigue them.

It was – and still is – a marathon, making Sunday lunch *pour toute la famille*. Soup, even on the hottest day, was *de rigueur*. The fields being awash with huge sun ripened tomatoes, tomato soup seemed an obvious choice and happily turned out to be Grandpa's favourite. As on the first occasion when they ate with us they all begged the merest taste of each dish before, reassured, returning for a second helping. To follow the soup I had simply whisked a large tin of red salmon with half a pound of melted butter, black pepper and the juice of two lemons, decorating it with cucumber and parsley, to be eaten with thin slices of *pain complet*. Raymond had never tasted wholemeal bread before and was not impressed but Grandpa, reminded of his days in Germany as a prisoner of war, enjoyed it and gave us lurid accounts of the bread he ate then. The salmon was declared *extra*, Grandma's highest praise.

All the morning I had hovered over the *gigot* in my crazy oven. To date no-one can explain to me the reasons for the different methods of heating in French and English gas cookers. I have peered into gas cookers, from the earliest ones at the new Gas Museum at Bromley by Bow, where I learned that the first experiments in cooking by gas were made by a Paris-trained chef in 1809, to the latest models in French hypermarkets, and the difference between them never varies. The gas jets are differently positioned and this results in the floor of the oven being cool in an English cooker. Not so in a French one. In my French cooker the gas jets are in the form of a ring similar to those on the top, but under the oven floor. They are lit through a small hole and the flames fan out sideways to make the floor of the oven extremely hot. There are two slender slots on each side of the oven floor presumably to allow the heat to rise, but I have found that a great deal of it seems to prefer to stay where it is. Hence the problem. It is clear to me that this is the reason that the French make superb, open tarts with crisp, firm bases and we make equally good, but different, pies with covered, golden-brown tops, but whether the tarts are the reason for the different ovens or vice versa, I have still to discover.

While the *gigot* was anxiously watched, removed, re-positioned and re-basted, I also attempted an approximation of roast potatoes, the local variety being so waxy and flavoursome. At the top of the oven they refused even to change colour. Exasperated I tipped them onto a foil covered baking sheet and put them at the very bottom. Oven-sautéed rather than roast potatoes were the result but constant turning made them brown rather than burn and they were a novelty to *les Bertrand* and eaten with relish. Three vegetables were eaten with the *rôti*: I had braised in butter tiny carrots and *navets*, a completely new idea − as was the mint sauce which Mike had made. Claudette, always more adventurous than the rest of the family, tried the sauce and quite liked it but Raymond would have none of it. The *gigot* however had clearly been a treat and we were pleased.

Salad, cheese and a passion fruit sorbet from the local supermarket was finally followed, for a joke really, by mince pies. We explained that normally they were only served at Christmas. 'What a shame! Only once a year,' murmured Raymond, as he reached for yet another one.

It was a happy lunch. Indoors it was cool, our metre thick walls protecting us from the blazing mid-afternoon sun which covered *le grand champ* in dancing heat haze. Grandpa taught us to say *fai calou* − it is hot, in patois. '*Fai calou!* he roared, the children copying him and giggling. Both grandparents are fluent in Occitan, the *langue d'Oc*, the ancient language of the Troubadours and the whole of southern France. When they talk to one another they use it most of the time. Raymond and Claudette understand but rarely use it, and the children are not really interested although there is, as with many old languages under threat, a revival of interest. Classes are held in the summer and there is a serious study of Occitan at Toulouse University – an event little dreamed of by the southern children of sixty years ago who, during their first weeks at school, were beaten for being unable to speak French.

Occitan is much more like Spanish or Italian and though the younger generation do not use it, their famous accent *du Sud Ouest* shows its influence as they invariably pronounce the final syllable as in Italian. Raymond told us the story of the Gascon, newly conscripted and stationed in the North. The expression on his face as he told it made it clear that it might as well have been the North Pole as anywhere north of the Loire. This Gascon is invited by a fellow soldier to visit *la mer* for the weekend. Accordingly, with keen anticipation, he packs his swimming trunks and towel only to find that his new friend has merely taken him home to meet his mother. Bitterly disappointed he cries, *'Mais – tu n'as pas dit LA MER-RE. Tu m'as dit LA MER!'*

Raymond told us about local customs. One in particular seemed to be concerned with newly-weds. It appeared that after the ceremony and wedding breakfast they did not disappear on their honeymoon but spent the first night nearby at a neighbour's house. 'Then,' explained Raymond, his eyes shining, 'Everyone must go round to find which house and then, in the middle of the night, they return to surprise them.' This seemed rather unsporting to me but it did not end there. The visitors take with them food and wine – after all it is a French custom – and also a huge pot of a soup called *le tourin* from which the whole affair takes its name, to *faire le tourin*, and the hapless couple have no alternative but to get up and begin the festivities all over again. 'Does this happen at every marriage round here?' I asked incredulously.

Raymond shook his head. *'Ca dépend des gens. Ce n'est pas toujours pour un mariage,'* he grinned. *'Ca pourrait arriver ici.'*

Towards the end of the following week when Tony was reluctantly considering the long journey back to the north of England, the temperature climbed every day until a *canicule* or heatwave was officially declared. The thermometer on our north-facing porch reached 93° that afternoon, and by midnight it had barely fallen. Crickets whirred in the hot still air and the moon was brilliant. We talked, as old friends do, and drank deeply while watching for satellites to pass in the vast, magical heavens. In a mad moment we decided on a moonlit stroll up past the pond to the brow of the hill. Laughing at some absurdity of Tony's we lurched somewhat unsteadily along and were rather surprised when Matthew suggested that we were much too drunk to continue and ought to be in bed. 'Out of the mouths of babes,' we thought, unaccustomed to such solicitude from our younger son. We should have known better.

About an hour later, deeply asleep and naked but for a sheet, which, I realised later as Raymond retold the story, barely covered either of us, we were awakened. Stupefied, we heard voices and footsteps close by and forcing open our heavy eyelids we saw what appeared to be half the village. Led by Raymond they laughed, sang and capered about our bedroom like characters in a painting by Brueghel. Coming from the kitchen were smells of food and the clink of bottles. Dear God! It was the dreaded *Tourin*. What were we supposed to do now?

We stumbled out of bed as onto a film set in action in which we had not the slightest idea of the script. Everyone else, it was clear, was thoroughly rehearsed and Raymond was the director. Clutching our flimsy dressing-gowns we were led from the bedroom. In a dazed dream I recognised the Mayor backing through my front door with a wooden bench covered in a tartan rug. I tottered to a seat as Simone, the mason's wife, began to unwrap a great dish of hot sausages. The tureen of soup was steaming on the table and a giggling Claudette scurried up and down laying cutlery and glasses, followed by a small dark woman with tight curls who turned out to be the Mayor's wife, setting the plates. Sitting in the chimney corner, could it be? Yes. It was the schoolmaster, his baby son on his knee. His wife was taking sponge cakes out of a basket, as if it were four o'clock in the afternoon. In staggered M. René and the insurance man with a carton of wine while people I hardly recognised ran back and forth with folding chairs and yet more bottles. As the whole scene rolled with a gleeful precision Grandpa sat himself formally at the head of the table, his watery old blue eyes alight with mischief.

A cheer greeted a befuddled Tony as he emerged from the other bedroom led by a triumphant Philippe and Matthew who had known all along. My tolerance to alcohol is low and I had already drunk far more than usual before going to bed but there was no way that night that more could be refused. The next few hours remain a boozy haze. I remember the soup, hot and full of garlic and bread with cheese melted on the top. It was wonderfully recuperative which was just as well for it was to be a long night. Even if one had started sober there was a routine to ensure that one did not remain so, especially the women who were, on the whole, very abstemious. An ancient drinking song, which may well be a medieval corruption of the Latin Mass, began the proceedings. They started on me.

'*Ami Rus. Ami Rus,*' they chanted.

'*Bois dans ton verre et surtout ne le renverse pas.*
Et porte le au frontibus, au nezibus, au mentibus
à l'aquarium, au sexibus. Et glou et glou et glou et glou . . .'
Then followed a great cheer as the glass was drained.

'*Elle est des nôtres. Elle a bu son verre comme les autres*
C'est une ivrogne. Ça se voit rien qu'à sa tronche.'
'Friend Ruth friend Ruth.
Raise your glass and above all don't tip it over.
And with it salute your forehead, your nose, your chin,
Your belly and your sex, and drink and drink and drink . . .
She's now one of us. She's drained her glass like the rest
She's a drunkard. It's obvious if you look at her face!'
No one escaped. the wine flowed as everyone drank the

77

toast. When it was Véronique's turn, the only virgin, the word *sexibus* was delicately omitted.

After the toast everyone sang, the Mayor, the schoolmaster and Grandpa who made his grandchildren laugh as he roared out old songs from the war without any recognizable tune. In a low, sweet voice Grandma sang an old ballad, *Le temps des Cerises* – cherrytime, which she has since taught me. Raymond kept yelling 'Chantez Rus, chantez.' I have no idea what I sang. My entire repertoire three times round I should imagine. Mike is not a great one for singing. He seemed to spend most of the time hanging on to the sideboard with one arm and holding me up with the other. I do not remember going to bed for the second time that night. Next morning, about midday, when we finally emerged with extreme care, there were forty-seven empty bottles on the table to explain why we felt so fragile.

Once again the holiday was almost over and we began the last minute organising of work that would, we hoped, be completed during the winter. We had decided to have the floor of the main room tiled in terracotta and the tiler agreed to come, although he lived some distance away, so that he could eat with his sister at midday. What a very French arrangement.

Later that week we paid a last quick visit to M. Albert the plumber, to pay some bills and to make the final plans for the bathroom. It was a glorious evening and we found him and his wife in their garden admiring their vines which grew as a pergola and were heavy with bunches of purple grapes. We told him of our midnight visitors of the week before and asked if such a thing happened in his village. He chuckled, 'Mais bien sûr.' He looked at us as though sad at our ignorance. 'Quand il y a du soleil,' he said, 'il y a de la joie!' When there is sunshine there is joy.

7

*B*ack in London we were to need that joy to support us in the coming weeks. At the end of September our younger son Matthew was involved in a traffic accident and spent three weeks in a coma. Hour after hour we sat by his bed talking to him incessantly, desperate for the slightest response, and much of our talking was inevitably about Bel-Air. Eventually he opened his eyes but we had been warned that there might be brain damage. A succession of his friends came, the ever faithful Durrell each day after school, and sometimes he would move one hand slowly as if in greeting before drifting back again into that world we could not enter. After several weeks the nurses would sit him up each day for an hour but all he did was stare into space. Was this how it would always be?

One day his father took in a sketch book and some bright, felt-tipped pens. Matthew, his head lolling forward, was propped in a chair.

'This is Matthew's get-well book,' said Mike, with a desperate cheerfulness. He drew on the first page. 'This is Matthew's get-well clown. He's called Fred. What's he called?' he shouted.

Matthew focused very slowly on his father. His mouth moved and a sound came out.

'What's he called?' Mike repeated.

'F-red,' croaked Matthew. The ward stopped. Frantically Mike turned the page to scribble another shape.

'This is Matthew's get-well caterpillar,' he said. 'What shall we call him?'

Matthew looked puzzled.

'Carbolic,' yelled the old man in the bed opposite. Sister came running down the ward. 'Well done,' she said to Mike, 'but that's enough for now.' She put our son back to bed and Mike phoned me at home. Later we sat by his bed. He was asleep. When he stirred we began talking to him. We planned the redecoration of his bedroom, a new carpet, bookshelves, the next trip to France – perhaps we might fly – we just kept on talking. Suddenly he opened his eyes and looked straight at us. 'Are-you-anticipating-my-being-in-here-a-long-time-then?' he intoned in a loud Dalek-like voice all on one note. We cried.

The get-well book progressed daily with ever more difficult concepts. There was Doris the Dotty Dotted Dalmation who was going for a walk in the opposite direction from her master. There were the Doctors. They're the Best in Town. The Problem is they're Upside Down. And there was the Zebra with Horizontal stripes. All the other patients in the ward waited for the next picture. We had been warned that Matthew's memory might be affected and so we brought in enlargements of photographs that we had taken that summer at Bel-Air.

Matthew had asked Philippe what the signs for BALL TRAP meant which we often saw in country lanes. He told us it was clay pigeon shooting and that he would show us how it was done. The village fête which had taken place before our arrival had included a contest in one of their meadows and afterwards Grandpa had collected up all the undamaged clay discs. We had borrowed the primitive launcher from the Mayor. A Heath Robinson-type contraption, it had been assembled by the local *mécanicien* using a metal seat from an ancient hay-rake and a large spring to catapult the discs. Matthew had had great fun using a twelve bore double-barrelled shotgun at the shout of 'PULL'.

'Who's that?' we asked him. He glanced at the photographs then smiled. 'It's me. Doing Ball Trap.' There were long weeks of physiotherapy to follow and hours of coaching for his 'O'levels, alas only a few months ahead. We had so much to be thankful for. But it was not over. On Christmas Day he almost died again; this time from anaphylactic shock, a massive allergic reaction to eating a walnut. It was completely unconnected with his accident. Although he had always suffered from allergic asthma we were totally unprepared for such a dangerous reaction and our sheer ignorance nearly cost him his life. By the time Easter came round once more we were all in need of the quiet peace of Bel-Air.

As though especially ordered to soothe our shattered nerves, we caught the full beauty of the plum blossom that spring. Every farm was *'en fête'*. Creamy white, flowering orchards patchworked the gently rolling hillsides of Lot-et-Garonne under the clearest of blue skies. Raymond has four such orchards and the highest one was especially beautiful, being carpeted with wild yellow tulips. The cuckoos called all day from the wood and we rejoiced to watch Matthew and Philippe walking together across the fields.

One morning Raymond took us into his cave to show us the great *barrique* in which he had put two hundred and forty litres of *vin de Pays*, the product of the now well-established *Cave Coopérative* at Monflanquin. Apart from making a small quantity of sweet white wine for the family, he now sent all his grapes to the *Coopérative* and sadly his *petit vin rouge, fabrication maison* was now a thing of the past.

'That barrel,' he said, patting it gently, 'is my best one. It's made of oak and once held *le vin noir de Cahors*. I shall leave this wine to mature in here for at least four years and then, you'll see, it will be something special. There are two hundred and forty litres there. Would you like to buy a half share?' Naturally we agreed.

He explained that each spring, *à la vieille lune de Mars*, which confusingly often falls in April, the wine must be taken out, the barrel washed, and the wine replaced. '*Ça c'est le nettoyage*,' he said. 'If you are here you can help me with it. And then of course, you'll have to decide, in four or five years' time that is, where you are going to keep all those bottles. All these alterations you are planning. Don't forget somewhere for your wine!' Slowly the house was beginning to take shape; as Grandpa always says, '*petit à petit, l'oiseau fait son nid.*' Little by little the bird makes its nest.

The living room seemed larger with its handsome, freshly-tiled floor. There was a wonderful variety of tone and I spent several hours on my hands and knees wiping each tile thoroughly with linseed oil as I had been instructed by the tiler. The new main bedroom was, as we had hoped, a splendid size and the ancient double window now included gave it added charm. We soon moved in and discovered to our delight that on a clear morning we could, sitting up in bed, see right down the valley. At other times we awoke wrapped in an eiderdown of early morning mists which the sun rolled slowly back, revealing first *le grand champ*, then a thread of smoke curling up from Grandma's chimney, next the church spire and finally the distant horizon, clear and sharp against the sky. We vowed never to plant anything that would obscure that view.

We were invited to *faire le tourin* again that holiday. Twice in fact; they seemed to have got the taste for it. On the first occasion it was M. René, the mason, who plotted to surprise Raymond and Claudette and the rendezvous was at his snug little house in the village. There we gathered soon after eleven to find Simone, his wife, busily preparing the soup and the sausages. There were shouts of welcome at each new arrival in the steamy kitchen.

Towards midnight we all crept along the road, collars turned up against a chill wind, the sky full of stars. Philippe, in the plot, had arranged to switch off the porch light when he judged his parents to be asleep. Across the crossroads, past the village shop, we carted the bottles and the bread, the piles of hot sausages and the huge pot of soup. There was consternation when, on arriving at the end of the village, we saw that Raymond's light still burned brightly. There was nothing to be done but to carry it all back again and play another game of cards.

Half an hour later, the light went out, and the whole operation began again. Muffling our giggles we tip-toed up the gravel drive with M. René, as excited as a child, organising everyone in a stage whisper. Up the steps we went and into the veranda room. There were subdued clinks as the food and drink were laid quietly on the table and in we crept in single file, through the inner corridor, past the ornate sideboard and the stuffed birds and into the bedroom.

Total propriety! Under an enormous quilt, Claudette wore her neat pyjamas, as demure as any track suit. After the first startled awakening they laughed and got eagerly out of bed. We all trooped back into the still warm kitchen and in a few minutes Claudette reappeared fully dressed, even wearing her flowered pinafore. As though it were midday plates and glasses were swiftly laid while Raymond disappeared into his secret *cave* for some of those dusty undated bottles of *vieux Cahors*. Not having had a *cave* when we had been so visited, and, in any case, not knowing the form, we had simply drunk what had been so generously provided. Now we began to learn the obligations of those visited.

The second occasion was at the end of that holiday. This time Raymond and M. René were joint instigators but it was Simone, M. René's wife, who provided the means of entry. She cleans the school and also cooks the dinners for the twelve pupils and she simply stole the key to the school house. Late the next night the headlights of the odd passing motorist through our mad village would have briefly illuminated a stealthy and laden cortege advancing up the silent street.

The door of the schoolhouse creaked alarmingly, as did the wooden stairs up which we climbed one behind the other, to surprise the schoolmaster and his wife in the flat above. It was, in fact, we who were surprised. The school master had been out at a reunion and had driven home just in time to see the last intruder slipping into his house. Guessing what was afoot he merely crept up the stairs behind us and had the last laugh at our astonished faces when we found his wife in bed alone. 'Just as well she was!' said M. René afterwards.

At Bel-Air, the old staircase removed, we could now see the size of our bathroom to be. M. René had cut a window through the meter thick wall and had put down the first layer of cement flooring. He had also enclosed the space at the end of the corridor for the inside lavatory. M. Albert had almost finished the plumbing and we went to choose a plain white bath and bidet, and from M. Brut we ordered a pine cupboard in which to set our handbasin. As soon as the floor was finished our bathroom could be fitted.

That summer we welcomed Philippe to London for two weeks before leaving for Bel-Air. *Il faut en profiter* being one of Claudette's maxims she had despatched her son to improve his already competent English and we were pleased to find him intrigued by everything and an easy guest. On his first morning he leapt up from the breakfast table with a cry at the, to him, unbelievable sight of five fat breasted pigeons browsing on my Clapham lawn. Without his gun he learned to watch them and one of my favourite memories is his astonished delight as the birds in St James's Park fed confidently from his outstretched hand. Once he was home however he soon reverted to the national pastime and this autumn he cheerfully spent days cramped in a treetop hide waiting to gun down a passing pigeon.

His observations on going to school with Matthew were interesting. He found the discipline incredibly lax yet the teachers less friendly and more distant. He also thought the uniforms bizarre. I have to admit that the easy elegance and

cleanliness of most of the schoolchildren we see in France
– even the satchels they carry and the mobylettes they ride
are stylish – contrast sadly with the drab, and inevitably
grubby, daily-worn uniforms of so many English pupils.

We decided to buy a small motorcycle for Matthew to give
him the same freedom as Philippe. Only 50cc, they can be
ridden at fourteen and, as there is no public transport
between thousands of French villages, they are essential.
While her brother was off with the rest of the gang
Véronique would often come up to the house to give me
a *dictée*. She marked severely. *'Une petite faute, un demi-point,'*
she would say firmly as she looked over my latest effort,
then her eyes would widen as her father's did. *'Mais, là,
ça c'est terrible!'* She enjoyed playing schoolmistress and it
was very good for me.

The bathroom was now installed and the dreams of
luxuriating in soft and scented water a reality. Its soothing
powers were even more appreciated when we were initiated
into the strenuous pleasures of the potato harvest. *'Demain,'*
announced Claudette, *'on ramasse les pommes de terre.'* At
eight-thirty next morning we joined the rest of the family
at the top of the wide sloping field in front of the house
where all the vegetables are grown. The air was fresh and
we wore the usual pullovers to be discarded as the sun
climbed. Heaps of sacks were distributed the length of the
four long rows of potatoes. Grandma and faithful Fernande
from the next village carried baskets and rakes. Fernande
wore her usual thick woollen socks and flowered overall.
Her face is even wider than M. René's and as she smiled
at me, her row of large uneven teeth made her look like
a friendly pumpkin lantern.

Raymond was already busy walking behind a slowly
moving tractor guiding the ancient, wooden-handled
plough-share. *'Venez,'* he shouted. *'Venoir voir. La charrue
d'autrefois.'* He has a real affection for implements from 'the
olden days'. He proudly showed the plough to Matthew
explaining that then it was pulled by an ox.

'I remember that,' shouted Grandpa, stomping down the

field in his straw hat, as though nothing would be done properly unless he supervised it. 'Not so fast! Watch what you're doing,' he yelled at Philippe, who was driving the tractor. As the blade moved through the dry tangle of potato plants the harvest appeared, pale, silvery and abundant.

'*Pas mauvais.*' Not bad, said Raymond picking up a large potato and rubbing it clean on his shorts. 'The biggest ones are always at the bottom of the field – they get more rain.' Once all the rows were turned we could begin.

Alternately squatting and bending to relieve either our backs or our legs we began at the bottom of the slope and without stopping worked upwards until midday. After the first hour I was tired but, as usual, determined not to be outdone by either Grandma or Fernande, I carried on and found that the fatigue soon disappeared. During the first half hour we were disturbed by the sounds of an engine in distress and clanking up the drive came the most disreputable old banger, with several lengths of scrap iron tied to the roof. It was hard to distinguish the driver as the car was crammed with what appeared to be more scrap metal. We glimpsed a dark face under a greasy beret, a cigarette hanging from the lower lip.

'It's M. Demoli,' said Raymond resignedly.

'Late as usual,' muttered Grandpa without looking up. This was the infamous husband of poor Fernande about whom we had heard innumerable tales. The couple lived in a two-roomed house in the next village which was easily identifiable by the heaps of rusting metal outside the door. They had no electricity, running water, or sanitation and it was a source of wonder as to how Fernande managed to keep herself so neat and clean. M. Demoli it was said, did not bother. We could not wait to see him.

As he ambled down the field shouting something unintelligible, his swarthy, unshaven face had a wicked, unrepentant air. His bare feet were filthy under his ragged trousers which were held round his waist with string. The pocket of his check shirt bulged with folded papers and a row of pens. '*C'est mon bureau,*' he told Matthew later, patting it proudly. Raymond introduced him with a mixture of embarrassment and affection and M. Demoli's bold eyes glittered. He was strong and lifted the heavy baskets with ease. He made bawdy comments about each oddly shaped potato and teased the rest of us for wearing shoes. 'You should work like me,' he cried. 'See how tough my feet are.' He pulled a pin from under his collar. 'Here,' he challenged, 'stick that in my foot.' Matthew, laughing, tried unsuccessfully to penetrate his black leathery sole.

We progressed slowly up the long rows, the filled sacks standing like monuments to our labour and we were intrigued by a small decorative beetle that we kept finding among the potato roots. It had a familiar look. Philippe told us that it was called a *doryphor*. Suddenly we remembered where we had seen this distinctive red and black striped marking. We were handling dozens of Colorado beetles! Raymond was astonished to learn that in England posters describing them as villains are displayed outside police stations and that sightings must be reported. His eyes gleamed. 'Now I know what to do about Madame Thatchaire,' he said. 'I'll send her some in a matchbox.'

The sun was fiercer now and we were all working more slowly, but the end was in sight. Raymond led the way, encouraging us. He recited a fable by La Fontaine. He knew it almost by heart and when he faltered, Grandma prompted him. It was all about hard work.

'*Un riche laboureur, sentant sa mort prochaine, fit venir ses enfants,*' he said in his slow, careful French. A wealthy farmer, sensing his death was near, called for his sons to give them this advice.

'Never,' he said, 'sell off this heritage that has been handed down to us. A treasure is hidden here. I do not know quite where, but with a little courage you will find it, in the end. Turn the soil as soon as harvest's over. Plough it, dig it, hoe it, leave not an inch unturned.' The father died. His sons worked every field, here, there and everywhere, so hard that in that year their yield was doubled. The treasure they could never find. Their father, wise old man, had shown them all before he died that it is work itself which is the treasure. '*Que le travail est un trésor,*' finished Raymond, his eyes shining. Listening to these words with aching limbs, my nostrils filled with the peppery sting of newly unearthed potatoes and the sun hot on my tired back, I felt a great shared satisfaction. Grandma and Fernande, raking the last few that we had missed, slowly brought up the rear and Raymond called, '*C'est fini. Allez, allez manger!*'

As usual Claudette had left the field some thirty minutes before us and was briskly laying the table as we came gratefully into the cool of the verandah room, each blind lowered against the heat outside. I heard her 'tut tut' as M. Demoli's black feet made marks all over the tiled floor and I knew that before she returned to work she would be busy with a mop. Matthew laughed as M. Demoli took off his greasy beret to scratch his head and two boiled sweets and three hand-rolled cigarettes fell onto the table.

Replacing the beret he handed us the sweets. We dared not look at one another as we thanked him and put them in our pockets. As soon as he had finished his soup he poured the wine into his bowl and, lifting it to his stubbly chin, drained it with noisy pleasure. This custom is called *faire le chabrot* but is more often seen on picture postcards. M. Demoli was an incorrigible entertainer. He unloaded his *bureau* to show us his *carte d'identité* and an old photograph of a stolid young woman. '*C'est ma fille,*' he cried, '*elle parle très bien l'anglais.*' We looked at Fernande for confirmation but she said nothing. She just ate and ate with a silent contentment the delicious dishes which Claudette provided.

The soup was, as usual, followed by melon and home-cured ham. Then came a *pâté de canard* with a small circle of her *foie gras* in the centre of each slice. Next she served a baked dish of rice and courgettes covered in cheese and finally, roast pork, green salad and, for dessert, *flan*, rather like cream caramel without the caramel, and highly flavoured with vanilla. By two-thirty, rested and revived, we rose from the table, the men to load the sacks while we remained a little longer in the cool to clear the dishes. Sure enough out came the mop to remove all trace of M. Demoli!

'*Maintenant c'est le triage,*' said Claudette, as we followed her across the courtyard. I could not imagine what we were to do next. As we came into the oldest barn where all the poultry have their ramshackle nesting boxes the remaining hens and ducks shrieked and clucked as they flapped out into the sunlight. Ahead of her Claudette shooed, like a miniature corps de ballet, the twelve smallest ducklings, shutting them safely in an inner sanctum behind the pigsties. The turkeys scolded plaintively as they skirted past us, picking up their feet with a disdainful precision and the three pigs snorted and squealed and trod on each other's feet. The whole barn was darkened by the bulk of the loaded cart drawn up at the entrance.

Suddenly Raymond appeared, staggering under the weight of a sack which he emptied onto a space which had been cleared at the far end. Onto the beaten earth floor tumbled sack after sack of potatoes until we had a great mound. Folded sacks were placed for us to kneel on and we began sorting them into baskets. *Le triage* was a simple but effective grading system. Everyone yelled instructions. '*Pour commencer − les plus grosses,*' shouted Raymond. He and M. Demoli swung up the filled baskets and carried them into an inner store where they were layered with a preserving powder to prevent rotting. Any bad potatoes were hurled to one side. After we had selected all the largest we progressed to *les moyennes*. From these we had to choose *les plus belles* for resowing the following season, the more ordinary went to be stored with the rest. It was surprising how quickly we demolished the heap until only the smallest potatoes remained. These, I learned were to be put into a box *pour les cochons*. I asked if I might take some for us. Raymond laughed. 'Have some bigger ones,' he said. He seemed surprised when I told him that I really did prefer them. Grandma smiled, 'She's right,' she said, 'they have the best flavour. They just take so long to peel.'

'We eat the skins as well,' I told her.

'It's possible,' she said politely. No sooner was the pile finished than Raymond fetched more sacks and we began again, kneeling in this cobwebbed and chicken-cooped, semi-darkness as generations before us must have done, on this same floor of beaten earth.

At last it was finished, the baskets banged against the wall and stacked inside each other, the sacks shaken and folded. Grandma swept the dust into the corner with a besom. Sensing the end of the invasion, one by one the chickens, calling softly, reclaimed their territory. Claudette took two still warm eggs from a nesting box and put them in her pocket. She emptied a basket of small potatoes for the pigs who squealed and scrunched with joy as we emerged into the blazing courtyard.

'*Alors*,' she smiled, '*Merci. Les pommes de terres sont ramassées.*'

8

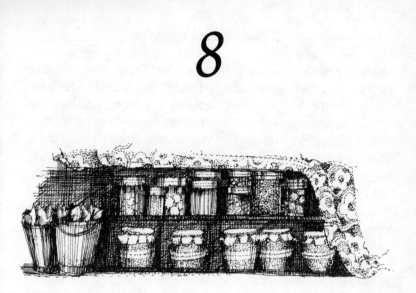

*T*hat summer we began to realise that we had a problem with rising damp at the front of the house and that it was getting rapidly worse. Wet patches appeared on the floor of the north-facing bedroom. They started at the outside edge and spread alarmingly across the entire room. Clearly something would have to be done, but what? We peered down the well. The water level was very high, might there be a seepage? We siphoned off gallons but still the damp persisted.

The following Easter things were much the same and we consulted M. René who, after prowling around for a few minutes, gave us the answer. The house had no damp course and therefore, he explained, the level of the soil outside was critical. Bel-Air, being on a gently sloping hillside, had acted, over the years, as a dam against all the soil which had been washed down. When we measured we found that the ground outside was a foot higher than the inside floor level.

'I think you really need a proper drive right round to the porch,' said M. René. 'I know the very person to dig it out for you. M. Mastero. He's Italian, but he's lived here for years,' he added reassuringly. Remembering his two other young workmen who had so quickly excavated the hole for the septic tank, I vaguely imagined a huge Italian who would do the work of two lesser men. Before the appointed Thursday I moved the kerria bush which, since the chopping down of the box trees, had struggled into bloom outside the north-facing bedroom window, and I dug up a few straggly marigolds and transplanted them into pots. About nine o'clock M. Mastero appeared in a small van. Five feet square, red-faced and very jovial, he did not look particularly energetic.

'It's not arrived yet then?' he cried.

'What?' we asked.

'*La pelle*,' he answered. We were perplexed. His shovel? Didn't he normally bring his shovel with him? Suddenly he looked down to the distant road. '*Ah elle arrive!*' he roared. Whatever he had seen had turned from the road onto the track far below us and was obscured by the trees, but we could hear a heavy engine and over the brow of the hill and into our disbelieving view came a lorry bearing a sign *CONVOI EXCEPTIONEL* and towering behind it a bright yellow mechanical digger. We had expected nothing like this. At that moment M. René's van appeared from the other direction and he tried to reassure us. '*C'est facile*,' he said. 'It's easy, one hour and it'll be finished.'

Now we began to understand the extent of the operation. The digger was almost as tall as the house and once it began to carve out a deep trench in a straight line from the track along the side of the house I realised I had a problem. I have an antipathy to straight lines, especially in gardens, and clearly *la pelle mécanique* and her handsome driver – M. Mastero was merely the owner – could neither comprehend or cut, it seemed, a curve. And so battle began.

A depth of at least two feet had to be dug to allow for a foot of stones to be laid as a soak-away for the water. Out came the old, romantic tunnel of vines which had so graced the side of the house. The japonica bushes staggered, collapsed, and were no more. Everything, without ceremony, was dumped into the back of the waiting lorry. Compared to my hours of effort with a small spade it was impressive, there was no doubt about that. But I now realised that a small syringa tree which stood at the corner of the house would be the next to go. I clasped my arms round it and defied *la Pelle*. 'Non! Non! Non!' I yelled.

The driver could not hear me but he could hardly miss my demented mime. He climbed down from his God-like height. M. René too came to see what was amiss. They all tried to persuade me. This tree and the next one, *une boule-de-neige*, were both in the way and would have to come down. Even Mike joined this male contingent of ravishers of my garden and, I felt, of Anaïs's too. I could plant other trees, they reasoned. I didn't want to. I was adamant. Why could *la Pelle* not go round them? Round was a silly word; she couldn't do anything round. Only square. Then could she not cut squares at the base of each tree? They looked doubtful. Perhaps, it might, just might, be possible. Not at all reasonable of course, but, perhaps, possible. Clearly they were not exactly eager to try. They shrugged, drew in their breath and looked at each other. They paced to and fro, wishing I had gone shopping.

'It would be difficult,' said the handsome young driver.

'But you could try?' I pleaded.

Maybe my tears of rage at the whole insensitive lot of them finally moved him but he climbed back up onto his machine and, of course, it *was* possible. It meant a lot of gear changing and backing and turning, but the ground was cleared right up to the house and my two small trees stood bravely up on their squares of earth, startled but safe.

When the lorry was full with earth the driver asked where he might dump it. The maize in *le grand champ* had not yet been sown and Raymond, who had by now arrived to watch the operation, said airily, 'You can dump it there on the edge of the field. I'll flatten it later.' I do not think he bargained for the twelve loads that were eventually excavated.

Once the edge of the house had been cleared the digger

went back to the track to widen the trench that he had cut. Everyone who drove to our front door swung naturally round in a curve but *la Pelle* of course, could only work in a straight line. Our proposed new drive and parking space grew ever wider and our meadow consequently smaller. Not needing to accommodate a fleet of lorries, we stopped him.

'Right,' he shouted. 'I'll just straighten this bit up,' gouging out yet another right angle. I have never been so glad to see the back of such a beautiful man.

The next day the stones were laid; eight inches of large stones beneath four inches of smaller ones. We raked them into place. The sun shone and the newness and whiteness of such a large area was horribly dazzling. Now it has mellowed with mosses and the wild flowers have returned. Honesty, love-in-a-mist and marguerites soften those hard edges. The days after the departure of the ravening digger I spent moving barrows full of earth back from the field to our garden in an attempt to change the straight lines into curves. Raymond teased me. 'You've just paid to have it all removed. Now you're putting it back again!' But when I rested he climbed down from the tractor and filled three or four loads for me, piling the barrow high and pushing it as though it weighed nothing.

That summer, in the rough ground at the top of *le grand champ* which, after the lorry had dumped our garden soil, Raymond had left uncultivated, we had a wonderful nursery of small plants. Encircled and protected by the maize in the remainder of the field, small japonica bushes appeared, daisies and hollyhocks, Chinese lanterns, marigolds, tansy and honesty, sweet william, balsam and golden rod; seeds that must have lain dormant in the earth close to the house, perhas that Anaïs herself had once planted, were now jolted into life. We spent hours transplanting them.

The syringa and the *boule-de-neige*, or viburnum opulus, that I had only just managed to save from destruction, were thriving and have grown more beautiful each succeeding year. This October I watched its leaves turning ever more

glorious shades of crimson and I was doubly glad that I had
saved it. And we have had no more problems with the
damp.

Raymond, our mentor in every local tradition, decided that
it was high time that we started our own *cave*. 'Why don't
you make use of the other pigsty next to the outside
lavatory?' he said. 'It faces north and should be ideal.' We
already had the old wine racks which we had found in the
attic so we gave them a coat of wood preservative before
installing them in the dark and cool little store. Now to
choose the wine, a serious business.

After numerous telephone calls to a variety of cousins,
Raymond arrived one afternoon in his oldest 2CV with a
medium sized barrel or *fût* hidden under some sacks. He
and Mike went off for an hour or two's *dégustation* in the
idyllic Lot valley, not far from Cahors. The first wine they
tasted was, at that time, selling for between four and five
francs a litre. Not entirely satisfied, and in any case, out
for the afternoon and intent on as wide a choice as possible,
they climbed further up into the hills for yet another tasting
and, for nine francs a litre, they knew they had found just
what they were looking for.

After cleaning it with a sulphur candle, the *producteur*
weighed their barrel, filled it with his finest wine and
weighed it again. The bill, which we shared, came to just
under a hundred pounds. Before they left, the *producteur*,
a meticulous man, recommended that they bottle it straight
away. 'Moi, je connais mon vin,' he declared. 'Mais je ne
connais pas votre fût!'

At last we had a use for all those dozens of empty bottles
that we had found everywhere, in the house, the attic and
the *chai*. We cleaned them thoroughly and took them in
cartons down to Raymond's cave where the precious *fût*
waited. Although the day was hot, once we had passed
beneath the low lintel we entered a world of dark, damp
and unchanging coolness. Our barrel was at the beginning
of a long row of barrels of various sizes, beyond which were

haphazard piles of crates and mysterious curtained cupboards, containing Claudette's famous preserves.

Raymond pulled aside the dusty lengths of a variety of fabrics to show me the dozens of jars of *foie gras* and *confit de canard* – joints of fattened duck preserved in their own juices and covered with a thick layer of duck fat – the pots of *pâté* and *rillettes*, the bottles of asparagus, beans – green and white, dark red cherries, golden peaches and fat white pears. How many more there must have been before the advent of the deep freeze! On the floor in the darkest corner sat old enamel buckets packed with chicory plants, some sprouting fat cream shoots, others newly cut. Such self-sufficiency and expertise was fascinating.

As we began to unload the bottles, Grandma, flowered apron over her thick cardigan, came to help us stack them neatly in front of our barrel to the left-hand side. To the right she arranged several wine-stained planks until she was satisfied that they would not tip on the uneven earth floor. At last she nodded, placed a small rush-seated stool in front of the barrel and calling, *'Venez, venez,'* she hurried outside.

The smoke gusted from her chimney as we followed her across the courtyard and through the narrow door into her primitive kitchen where a large iron cooking pot bubbled on a wood fire. She lifted the lid to show me the dozens of corks bobbing in the steamy water. *'Il faut l'emporter à la cave, Michel,'* she indicated. She took a very long-handled shovel from behind the door and once Mike had lifted off the pot she scooped a heap of the hottest ashes and trotted ahead of us across the courtyard back into the cave where she dropped them in the far corner and helped to lower the pot on top. She explained that as we used the corks we must add others and that the water must remain warm. *'C'est le système,'* she smiled. Grandma has a *système* for almost everything.

She squatted on the stool, turned the tap on the barrel and the bottling began. Each filled bottle she handed to me, and I became part of *le système*, standing each one carefully on the planks within easy reach of Mike and Raymond who banged in the corks which would later be sealed with wax. Naturally we had to make sure that the wine was still good and inevitably we spilled a little from time to time. The whole cave smelled of *Cahors* and wood smoke and, crouching to avoid cracking one's head on the low, beamed ceiling, it was a strange, troglodite experience. After we had filled some one hundred and fifty bottles we were quite glad to emerge and straighten up in the warm brightness outside but we were also very pleased to think that our *cave* had really begun.

We labelled our odd assortment of reclaimed bottles Cahors '79, and proudly arranged them in our crudely-made wine racks. Later that year Raymond telephoned us in London to say that he had the opportunity to buy a *fût* of Corbières and would we like to share it. So another sixty litres of good red wine went into our cobwebbed pigsty. The only problem we have is keeping it long enough to reach its full maturity.

That summer, Adam, our elder son, sounding more than usually depressed on the telephone, said that he thought a visit to Bel-Air, which he had never seen, might be just what he needed. Delighted, we went to Bordeaux to meet him and were shocked to see how thin and unhappy he looked. Clearly all was not well. In the days that followed we watched the space and calm of our house in the sun begin to put him together again. The unreal world of rock and roll receded as he collected wood and mended fences with Raymond who treated him with a kindness and sensitivity I shall always remember. Claudette did her best to fatten him up, his French improved daily and he and his brother got to know each other better.

More friends arrived. Graham Bishop, a wonderful craftsman, alas by then too ill to carry stones himself, patiently taught me how to build a low, dry-stone wall to edge my now happily curved flower-bed which faced the porch. I learned to weigh the stones in my hand to balance them and to turn them until they sat naturally. It was fascinating work.

While Graham and Adam played chess under the great ash tree we decided that it was time that we at least attempted to clear the *chai* or outhouse. We needed room to store our growing collection of tools, ladders, tins of paint and wood preservative, garden furniture and the bicycles which we intended to bring next time. Most of the barrels in the *chai* were rotten and they disintegrated as we moved them. The two which remained we sawed in half and planted with marigolds, honeysuckle and marguerites, hoping they would look after themselves. And so they have.

Again we found the strange wooden, sledge-like object that had originally been in the attic. What on earth could it be? Grandma laughed when we asked her. She dusted it off with a cloth and carried it into the bedroom. Lifting the covers she slid the pointed end into the bed. Now we understood. The curved shape held the covers high and the hook in the centre was to suspend a metal lined box full of hot ashes. It was called *la moine*. Why she did not know. She also found a larger metal-lined box called *un chauffe-pied*. These she told us were used by the old ladies *d'autrefois* – in the olden days – to keep their feet warm. They put them under their long skirts when they sat shelling walnuts. It was clear that we had a great many fascinating things just lying around the house.

Mike and Matthew carried out an ancient winnowing machine. Raymond came to explain how that worked. It was first used around 1880 and was the earliest mechanical aid for stripping the chaff from the wheat. As the grain was slowly tipped into the top of the machine it was separated by contact with the wooden blades of a paddle wheel which was turned by hand. It made a whirring sound and the name in patois was *le tarare*. When pronounced with the Italian *r* it was a very descriptive name. Raymond insisted that we put it safely in his barn. It was something *d'autrefois* and rightly to be preserved. In fact they never threw anything away.

The more we cleared the *chai* the larger it seemed. It could clearly be made into a beautiful room, perhaps a studio. The walls were especially beautiful: apart from the highest wall which adjoined the house itself, they had never been plastered and were a wonderful example of *pierres apparentes*. The high wall had once been roughly rendered with earth and also contained several large, worrying cracks and we thought that it might be prudent to ask M. René to cement it when he cemented the floor that winter. He agreed and chalked on a board which was nailed to the wall: *CREPIS CE MUR.*

One morning Matthew came in very excited. 'You'll never guess what Philippe and I've been doing,' he cried. 'Grandpa's got this old car –'

'Grandpa has nothing *but* old cars, vans and that old 2CV –'

'No! No! *Really* old. A 1929 Citroen. It's in a barn behind the church. It's been there ever since the war. He hid it from the *Germans!*' Matthew was wide-eyed.

By now we were all interested. 'Philippe says he's going to ask him if we can get it out.'

Later that afternoon we went to look. Raymond and Grandpa led us to a barn that we had never even noticed before. Tucked behind the church, the huge doors creaked as we pushed them slowly open. Inside was a museum. Ancient farm machinery, wooden carts with great high wheels and oxen yokes attached, a pony trap and, hidden behind them all, covered with sacks, gleamed the dark green body of the old Citroen. It had Grandpa's name on the back and the original tyres with DUNLOP clearly marked on the spare wheel. 'Has it really been here since the war?' we asked.

The old man nodded. 'We hid her from the Germans,' he shouted triumphantly. 'We were supposed to give up all our vehicles but they never found mine.'

'But why didn't you get her out afterwards?'

'He shrugged. 'I don't remember. I hadn't the time. There was too much to do and anyway petrol was short.'

'Can we get her out now, Grandpa?' begged the boys.

He looked at the car. 'If you want to,' he said and then without another word he turned abruptly and walked off. I watched his small figure trudging back to the house and wondered what memories he was recalling.

Eagerly the boys uncovered her to reveal her high stately shape. 'She's just like in "Bonnie and Clyde",' said Matthew. They jacked her up to remove the wooden blocks on which she had rested and pumped up the tyres which astonishingly stayed hard. She would not start, however, that had been too much to hope for.

'I'm afraid the motor's seized up,' said Raymond sadly. However, Claudette's cousin, who kept the garage in a neighbouring village arrived the following morning and a small crowd assembled to watch as, pulled by the tractor, she began slowly to emerge from obscurity after almost forty-five years.

The cousin towed her away to see if it were possible to revive her. Two hours later he telephoned to say that he had a problem. He needed a new cylinder head gasket and, if we could find it, a radiator cap. For a 1929 Citroen? Raymond scratched his head. He had heard that there was a specialist in old cars somewhere near Villeneuve and off we went, none too hopefully, to see whether he could help us.

In several acres of ground which stretched down to the river Lot we found a tall, dishevelled, gentle man who ran a nursing home for hundreds of old cars, the most precious wrapped in old eiderdowns. While he wiped his hands – he had been restoring the body work of an ancient racing car – we explained what we needed. He said nothing. We followed him into a long shed and from one of a line of various wardrobes he took a bundle of cylinder head gaskets tied with elastic, and from a biscuit tin he handed us the radiator cap. He took our money courteously and then squatted down again to continue with his work.

Claudette's cousin grinned when he saw what we had brought and late that evening, the old car leading, we drove home in triumph and she's been running ever since. Mike loves to drive her, enjoying the challenge of the crash gear box and, when he's in a good mood, Grandpa will reminisce about *autrefois* when he first bought his car and he and Grandma were young. Now he prefers something better sprung and less draughty and leaves the Citroen to others.

Grandpa had told us that we were entitled to one free load of stones from the commune for our track up to Bel-Air every two years, and so far we had done nothing about it. However, thinking about the price we had paid for stones for the drive at Easter, we decided that now, while the track was dry, might be a good time to ask for them.

Unlike Raymond's farm, we learned that Bel-Air was just inside the border of the next commune and it was to meet a new M. *le Maire* that we drove on a Tuesday morning – that being the only time he was in his *bureau*. Raymond had advised me to go with Mike and I soon saw why. Our Mayor was a lady's man. Bronzed and handsome, he rose from his desk and in one swift stride enveloped my hand in both of his. His smile with a flash of gold fillings warmed me from head to foot.

'*Bien sûr*,' we could have the stones. He wrote the chit with a flourish. It was such a pleasure to meet us. He was absolutely delighted that the house was being restored.

A few days later he came to call. He was most affable, admiring all our renovations. It was he who explained the purpose of yet another curiosity which I had found and had hung on the porch. It was a metal ring about eight inches in diameter from which were suspended eight skewer-like objects with a hook at the end. But for hanging what? He laughed. He turned it horizontally, spreading out the skewers like tentacles. '*C'est pour la lessive*,' he cried.

Another search in the ever-open dictionary and we understood. It was to prevent the washing from boiling up out of the pot. The eight hooks clipped round the rim. The Mayor laughed. 'My mother had one,' he said. '*C'est quelque chose d'autrefois*.' We certainly didn't need to look *that* up.

9

Whm we arrived the following Easter almost the first thing we did was unlock the *chai* to see how it looked with its newly cemented floor and high wall. This was our worst moment so far. For some reason, which will perhaps forever remain a mystery, M. René or his workmen had ignored the high end wall so clearly marked *CREPIS CE MUR*, which so badly needed attention and they had, instead, covered each of the other walls of beautiful stones with cement. I could not bear to look. I closed the door and wept in the garden.

There seemed no point in asking him why he had done it. He had become a friend and would have been upset and, more to the point, there was no way it could be undone. I tried not to think about it and, gradually, I have forgotten just how lovely the walls once were. It was our first and, so far, only major disaster and it taught us not to leave important work to be done when we are not there. At least, not by M. René!

Fortunately, the next day was the last of *la vieille lune de*

Mars and time for *le nettoyage*. Our two hundred and forty litres of good red wine, maturing in the Cahors-flavoured oak barrel had to be scented, tasted and put into another barrel while the oak barrel was washed out, a happy distraction. Raymond rolled the substitute barrel outside onto the grass. He dusted it and, inviting us to stand close and watch, filled it with water. As he had anticipated it leaked on all sides, spraying us and amusing him. We patched the leaks with putty and topped it up. 'We can leave it now to swell,' he said.

In the veranda room he tipped the sleeping cats off the chairs. '*Autrefois*,' he said, measuring out the *pastis*, 'when we harvested the grapes, we would have to start washing out the barrels at least eight days before. We only put a little water in the barrel, we left it overnight then turned it to test the other side. *A la vôtre!* With twenty or thirty great barrels to do,' he continued, 'you couldn't possibly fill them all. It would take too long and use too much water. People didn't have water on tap then – you had to fetch it and so –' He turned his hand over, fingers limp and shook them in that unmistakably French gesture, '*Figurez-vous le travail!*'

The following afternoon we went down to help with *le nettoyage*. The barrel did not leak. It was emptied and positioned in the cave next to our special oak barrel. Now to fill it with the precious wine. Raymond put a large, wine-stained wooden tub beneath the bung of the full barrel and a funnel in the top of the empty one. '*C'est le moment*,' he shouted, his eyes sparkling. With two swift blows he knocked out the bung and the wine gushed out. 'Oh,' he cried, pulling a mock face, '*Ça sent mauvais*.'

'*C'est pas vrai*,' we yelled.

He laughed. '*Non, ça sent bon*.' He dipped a glass in the wine and we tasted. It was as good as it smelled and a wonderful, clear red.

Mike had to scoop the wine from the wooden tub with a small bucket and pour it into the funnel, working fast enough to prevent the tub overflowing. 'Do you need another bucket?' I called.

'*Non*,' Raymond replied. '*C'est notre système*. The wine is alive and must be disturbed as little as possible,' he shouted over the cascade, as he inserted a piece of wood beneath the far end of the barrel, tipping it gradually to ensure that the flow of wine did not stop nor the barrel tip back. As the wine began to flow more slowly we watched anxiously for any sign of deposit. '*Doucement, doucement*,' called Raymond. 'Is it still clear? I can't see properly from back here.'

'*Ça va*,' we shouted. '*Et alors, ça va.*' He lowered the barrel which although empty was still heavy and he and Mike staggered outside to wash it out. There was almost no deposit and Raymond praised the filtration sytem at the *Cave Coopérative*. '*Autrefois*,' he said, '*C'était plein de peau et de tout.*' It was full of skin and all sorts.

Once the barrel was completely clean they struggled to replace it securely in the cave. Ancient floors of beaten earth are not the most even and each old piece of wood he selected to correct the slope seemed more warped than the previous one but at last Raymond was satisfied. '*Là!*' he gasped. He replaced the lower bung and lit a sulphur candle which he suspended into the top of the barrel. The pale whisps of sulphur smoke which curled from between the slats made us sneeze and we reeled out into the fresh air until it had burned out. 'Philippe won't be very pleased when he comes home,' chuckled Raymond. 'His room is directly above and it seeps through the floorboards.'

'He'll have to sleep with his window open,' I teased.

'*Jamais*,' cried Raymond. They are as astonished that we sleep with our windows and shutters open as we are that they sleep with everything closed. Perhaps the proximity of their animals has something to do with it.

The barrel disinfected with sulphur, the whole process began again in reverse. This time there was no problem about disturbing any deposit. The wine frothed as it was poured back.

'In another three years this will be *formidable*,' promised Raymond. 'It already has a little *goût de Cahors*, don't you agree!' We all had another taste just to make sure.

That summer we were inundated by toads. During the day they hid motionless in corners, crouched behind the refrigerator, under the broom or in the wheelbarrow. As dusk fell they emerged in search of food. Their promenade was always in the direction of the pond where, I assume, there were more insects. We watched them pass, dark plodding lumps, totally unperturbed by anything in their path. If you kept still they would walk, cold and heavy, right over your foot.

Adam, our elder son returned. Bel-Air, we were pleased to see, had become a part of his life too. He spent several days in the attic wiring the rest of the house. It was a great pleasure to be able to read in bed. As a present he had brought a spotlight which he sited discretely on the porch, angling it to illuminate our bottle collection. There were those bottles marked CAIFFA and I still did not know what they had contained. Larousse simply stated that Caiffa was the ancient spelling of Haifa. Once again it was Grandma who gave us the answer. Caiffa was a company, a little like Kleeneeze, with travelling salesmen. It was based in Paris and sold almost everything, and gave stamps with each purchase. Another search in Anaïs's hat box produced a catalogue. *Les Etablissements de Caïffa* for 1927. Grandma turned the pages nostalgically. 'I remember when the Caiffa man came on horseback,' she said, 'with all his wares in two great pannier baskets. We used to run to meet him. How we looked forward to his coming.'

Many of the bottles had contained Seidlitz powders and Anaïs had also kept a small brochure written in 1933 by Doctor Berchon, whose precept for a healthy life was as follows: *Il suffit d'avoir la tête fraîche, les pieds chauds, et le ventre libre*. All you need is a cool head, warm feet and an uncluttered stomach.

After giving a lurid description of the dangers of self-poisoning by constipation, the learned doctor continues by extolling the virtues of *Le Seidlitz Charles Chantaud* which should be taken by anyone wishing to achieve an advanced age. It certainly seems to have done Anaïs no harm as she lived to ninety-two. A combination of magnesium sulphate, tartaric acid and bicarbonate of soda, it was said to purify the blood. M. Chantaud's success lay in his having found a way of transforming the remedy into granules which, packed in glass bottles would, unlike mineral water, keep indefinitely. 'For thirty years,' continues the enthusiastic Dr Berchon, *'Le Seidlitz Chantaud* has helped to cure migraine, gout, rheumatism and piles. From the salon to the theatre. At the ball. In the shop or studio it is now pronounced the King of Laxatives!'

That summer I began to work in earnest on my south-facing terrace outside the main bedroom door. The last strand of chicken wire removed and the ground fairly level, the problem had been the waist-high weeds which seemed to take me all the Easter holiday to clear, only to be back even more thickly when we returned in July. At last I did what I should have done to begin with, and weed killer and black plastic had resulted in a beautifully bare patch of ground. My terrace could now begin to take shape.

M. René tried to convince me to pave it with *des pierres d'Allemagne*, a machine-cut paving which is quite pleasing and has the advantage of being level. I, forever stubborn and in any case unimpressed by his aesthetic judgement, wanted to create a terrace which would look more integral with both the house and the garden. I had seen old terraces made of the local *pierres du Lot* and that was what I wanted.

A few kilometres outside the village M. René stores his building materials. Yes, he did have some of the great stones, if that was what we wanted. He explained to me how to cut them with a hammer and cold chisel and how to bed them in sand. *'C'est du travail!'* he said. I couldn't wait to start. Back and forth we went with the van, disturbing the basking lizards as we loaded sand and stones. You could tell at once which stones would split and where to place the chisel, and many of them contained fossils. Apart from helping me collect the materials Mike left me to it, thinking I would never finish it. My terrace took me three holidays to complete and I enjoyed every moment. I filled all the rough joins with a pale cement containing plenty of lime and smoothed it to leave the stones standing proud. I curved the edge into the grass and now it looks as though it has always been there. Of course it will never be as level as if I had used prefabricated slabs and each year I must repair a few joins or remove the odd weed, but my *pierres du Lot* are beautiful and change colour to a soft rose-beige when it rains.

My worst enemy in the garden is *la taupe*, the mole. Watering our grass simply provides him with damp earth in which to frolic. My lawn reduced to an uneven sponge, he finds himself beneath the terrace where he carelessly hurls up a stone or two before careering on under the flowerbed. Grandpa, muttering, sets his traps to no avail and I console myself by letting the mole do the digging and using the earth he provides to fill my flowerpots.

This summer our *campsis radicans* or American Trumpet Creeper, which two years previously we had planted as a straggly small shrub against the south-facing wall, finally climbed to the roof and we counted thirty-five scarlet blooms. I wonder why this spectacular climber is not more common in England as it can survive extremely cold winters.

On warm evenings in high summer, after eating outdoors on whichever side of the house takes our fancy, we sometimes stroll down the track and turn into the lane which winds to the village. The heat still rises from the tarmac and in the shrilling of crickets we eventually arrive opposite the church where the old ladies sit. All grandmothers, except poor Thérèse who lives in the Presbytery and must wear a wig for she is bald, they talk of gardens and grandchildren. Thérèse suffers from an incurable disease rather like leprosy and her deformed hands must be dressed each day by the nurse. Gaunt, mutilated, but uncomplaining she sits between the others as they discuss le *kiwi* which Mme Laval has planted this year. It will be three years before it fruits and we know whether or not it was a good idea. '*On verra,*' Mme Laval shrugs and smiles, '*et comment ça va les fils?*' They always want to know how Adam and Matthew are. Usually someone is knitting for a new baby. '*Bonne nuit,*' they chorus sweetly as we at last continue up the street to visit M. René.

His door is open and Simone, his wife, is shelling white beans for bottling. They are called locally *les cocos* and her washing-up bowl is almost full with these gleaming pearls, every shade from palest green to a subtly mottled silvery white. Delicious, especially in a tomato and onion sauce, the aftereffects are sadly the same as with all beans, what Grandpa calls *la musique des pauvres!*

In a chair by the open door sits M. Benoît waving both arms in a flurry of greeting. He is seventy-four but looks much older, with baby soft, silvery hair which fluffs from under his beret, and a toothless smile. The watery blue eyes widen when he sees that we have brought sweets and he takes one eagerly in his long, pale fingers, flat and so soft with beautifully shaped nails. Making breathy high-pitched sounds he sucks the fruit jellies noisily. He smiles. He wants to thank us but cannot and suddenly his eyes fill with tears. M. Benoît is dumb but not deaf. Born into a time and place where speech therapy was unheard of, he gave up trying to talk when his early efforts were ridiculed. Unmarried, he lived alone in a small house just outside the village where he cultivated a patch of land and was independent until his health and strength at last failed.

It was then that M. René and his wife took him in under an agreement called *rente viagère*. It is, in effect, a life annuity contract still quite common in rural France. An old person without relatives to care for them may make a contract with a friend or neighbour to be looked after and supported financially until they die, in exchange for their property. When I first heard of it I wondered whether it might be open to abuse, but as Mme René said, 'if anything were to happen to old Benoît I would be the first suspect.'

One evening when Raymond had just finished harrowing

le grand champ, relaxing at Bel-Air, *Pastis* in hand, he told us that it was exactly by such a contract that he had acquired our house and land. Anaïs, then almost ninety, had come with her son, himself in his late sixties, to ask Grandpa if he would consider such an arrangement. With no running water and their only heating the great open fireplace, which meant the constant cutting and carrying of wood, they no longer had the strength to care for land and livestock. Their only relative, a niece, was herself already looking after aged parents and parents-in-law. Grandpa agreed but asked them to wait until the following year when his daughter would marry Raymond and then the young couple would sign the document. And this they did. Seeing that I was very interested Raymond brought me the agreement to look at. It was the sheer practicality of it that impressed me. At that time, 1961, the house and all the land – vineyards, woods, fields – had been valued at 14000 francs. Raymond and Claudette paid 4000 francs and then agreed to supply annually:

fourteen hectolitres of wheat at each harvest

three barrels of 220 litres of red wine

a pig of 100 kilos live weight at *carnaval*

200 kilos of potatoes

4 cubic metres of firewood in September

50 Faggots

enough barley, oats and maize for 12 fowl.

The old couple kept the right to all the fruit and vegetables but not to sell them, and at the end was the most succinct detail of all: 'It is agreed that all these items shall be halved on the death of one, except the firewood.' I don't know how the chicken managed! Raymond paid the rates and taxes and Anaïs did not need to worry about her handicapped son. She died two years later.

One can only imagine how lonely and isolated Alaïs must have felt after his mother's death. For many years he had suffered with ulcerated legs and he now neglected them until he was obliged to go into hospital for lengthy treatment. Once there he became frailer and decided to remain. Each Sunday Raymond took him his week's supply of wine and tobacco and anything else he needed, and when the weather was fine he would bring him up to Bel-Air to sit in his favourite spot, looking southwards down to the distant hills on the far side of the river Lot.

In 1968 he died and was buried at his mother's side in the hill-top churchyard in the next village. Raymond and Claudette, young newly-weds, took over the land, the woods and the vines, the barn and the pond. But the house was closed and left to the spiders to wreathe in cobwebs, and the mice to nibble in the attic. For the next eight years it quietly gathered dust waiting for us to bring it back to life.

10

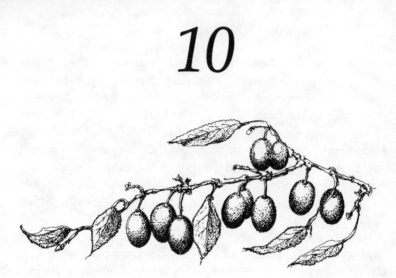

One hot afternoon, the box in the village being out of order, I went to the farm to use the phone. My number was engaged and while I waited talking to Claudette I was about to lean on the table behind me when I was stopped by a great shout and throwing up of hands. Looking round I realised that what I had taken to be a white tablecloth was in fact a covering of the thinnest of pastry pulled out and left to dry. I had almost caused a major disaster.

'*C'est pour la tourtière*,' laughed Claudette, the danger averted. We had seen these splendid almost sculptured apple pies in the *pâtisserie* and at the farmers' markets but a price of between six and seven pounds each had stopped us actually trying one. '*Venez voir*,' she said. In the kitchen was another equally long table already covered with a floured cloth. As though making a television programme she took a lump of soft dough from a box in the refrigerator and said, 'I shall start this one while I'm waiting for the other one to dry.'

Sprinkling a little more flour on the cloth she then lifted the supple dough. She put it across her upturned palms and wrists and, like an expert juggler, raised them alternately while gradually moving them apart. When the pastry was about two feet long she laid it gently down in the centre of the table calling, 'Eh, Oh!' over her shoulder. In an instant Grandma appeared to help her. *'Doucement! Doucement!'* she said softly as together they began to pull the pastry outwards to the edges of the table. Round and round they moved in harmony, Grandma clicking her tongue and muttering in patois when the smallest of holes appeared.

Twenty minutes later the long farm table was completely covered and the pastry hung several inches over the edge. Grandma trimmed it. 'The edge is far too thick to be used,' she said. 'Now we must leave it to dry.'

'For how long?' I asked.

'Usually an hour and a half. It depends on the temperature and the humidity. Now we can continue with the other one.'

The pastry on which I had almost sat was now transparent enough to show the white cloth underneath. Grandma appeared satisfied. She lined a large round baking-tin with foil and used a turkey feather to oil it. Then she dipped the feather into a small enamel saucepan of melted butter and covered the whole surface of the pastry. 'You've missed a bit over there,' cried Claudette.

Grandma sighed and moved round the table. 'My eyes are not what they were,' she said. She sprinkled the pastry with fine sugar and poised her knife for the first cut.

She removed a circle large enough to cover the base and sides of the tin, then put in three more, one on top of the other with the edges placed deliberately to look a little haphazard. She carefully arranged thick slices of raw apple over the base and sides, and then fourteen large sugar cubes were evenly spaced between them.

'Couldn't you use powdered sugar?' I asked, puzzled.

'Certainly, but fourteen lumps is our *système*.' Grandma was definite. I should have known better than to ask. Claudette sprinkled on a packet of vanilla sugar and then poured in two small tumblers of liquid. These were *eau-de-vie* and rum, each glass being diluted with an equal quantity of water. Circle number five was placed on next and then came the fascinating decoration.

They cut the remaining pastry into small shapes: strips, squares, triangles – *'n'importe'* – and, working from the outer edge, they folded and curved the pieces, standing them up to gradually cover the entire surface. They worked in absorbed excitement, like children on a beach, until with little sighs they stood back to admire their creation.

'Pas mauvais,' they grinned at one another. Grandma gave it a final sprinkling of sugar. I noticed there were still some pieces left.

'Plus tard,' said Claudette, anticipating my question. She explained that the pie must be cooked for fifteen minutes at gas mark 6, a further half hour at mark 5 and then those last curls would be piled even higher before the final fifteen minutes in the oven. 'Sometimes it works better than others,' she said, 'you'll be able to judge for yourself tomorrow.'

We had already been invited for Sunday lunch. 'Nothing special,' Claudette had said, 'just a few friends and some of the family.' But we'd never had *la tourtière* before. Was she sure they weren't celebrating something? 'No,' she laughed, 'I just felt in the mood.'

The next day the sun was even hotter and what little breeze there had been the previous day had dropped. At exactly twelve-thirty we drove down to the farm and joined a leisurely gathering in the flowered courtyard. Raymond was serving *apéritifs* to two town cousins and their children and to Grandma's jolly brother and his wife. He paused to introduce us to the only people we had not previously met, the local taxidermist and his ample wife.

In flowered aprons Claudette and her mother appeared for a brief ritual kissing and then hurried back to the kitchen. After a single aperitif we processed expectantly into the dining room on the veranda. Clearly this was not to be just an ordinary Sunday lunch. Our names had been written on torn scraps of paper and placed in the soup plates. RUHT, clearly they find my name as difficult to spell as to pronounce. We eventually settled, picked up our napkins and smiled at each other.

'*Servez-vous! Servez-vous!*' called Claudette from the far end of the table. The taxidermist's wife was quick to oblige. The soup was a thick *bisque de crevettes* and there were immediate murmurs of approval. Once it was finished and the plates collected by Véronique the first wine of the meal was poured. It is *deféndu* here to drink wine before soup. There was a glass of local red to start and then a Sauterne '76 to accompany the *foie gras entier de la maison* which followed.

'*Fai calou!*' agreed the old folk in patois and it was indeed hot even for early August. The small, thick creamy pieces of duck liver were eaten with an intense pleasure and compared favourably with last year's. Next came huge slices of my favourite Charentais melon from the garden. I watched Grandpa sprinkle his with salt and take the first bite from the end of his personal folding knife.

'*Oui, c'est bon,*' he declared. It was delicious and just the thing to cleanse the palate before the next course, a careful arrangement of *oeufs farcis* and curls of smoked salmon on a bed of tiny vegetables in mayonnaise, with which we drank a very dry Côte de Duras. What next we wondered.

'*Moi, je mange trop de pain,*' sighed Raymond reaching for another slice as Grandma carefully carried to the table a shallow tureen, steam rising from the dark aromatic sauce. This was our first experience of a *civet de lièvre*. It had been made from a hare shot by Grandpa and the flesh fell from the bones. It was extremely rich and thinking about the *tourtière* I took a very small helping. We drank a red wine from the *Cave Coopérative* at Monflanquin, which seems to improve every year since it first opened in 1978. In the kitchen Claudette was busy carving a huge *rôti de boeuf*. She piled up the thick slices and surrounded them with a great quantity of *haricots verts* which were gleaming with oil and dotted with garlic, while Raymond dusted off a hand-made bottle without a label. Eyes widened.

'What is it?'

'*Un vieux Corbière.*' He tried to look nonchalant but failed. The excitement mounted.

'*Mais de quelle année?*'

He shrugged. '*Je ne pourrais pas le dire.*' He turned to Grandpa. '*Quarante-huit? Quarante-neuf?*' The old man nodded. It was he who had bottled it when he returned from the war. The Corbières was a dark brownish red. It gleamed and was wonderfully smooth and was savoured with reverence. The beef was wonderful too. A town cousin, his chin glistening, asked if it came from one of the farm cows. 'Of course,' Raymond answered with pride. 'Don't you mind?' enquired one of the children. He shook his head, smiling at the boy.

After a simple green salad Claudette, to many oohs and ahs, carried in the *tourtières*, this superb south-west France version of an apple pie which I had so nearly ruined the previous morning. They were masterpieces, the golden curls of tissue thin pastry standing five inches high. We all applauded.

'*C'est ma fantaisie,*' said Grandma modestly. This tiny, tough old lady who can drive a tractor, kill a duck and harvest in the field with the strongest has little enough opportunity for *fantaisie* in her busy life. The pastry melted in the mouth and the interior was soft, sweet and extremely alcoholic. But we had not finished. *Sorbet de cassis* was in its turn followed by bowls of peaches and apricots and we drank our last wine, sweet and golden and made from the family vines on the hills above Bel-Air which had once belonged to Anaïs and her son.

When the coffee was finally poured into the tiny Limoges cups it was almost four-thirty and still the conversation rolled around the table. We struggled to understand as much as possible but were defeated when the old people slipped into patois. As we were offered *digestifs* there were impassioned discussions of the relative merits of Armagnac *haut* or *bas*, and the town cousin tried a Calvados brought back from a visit to the dreaded area north of the Loire.

Raymond refused to touch it complaining bitterly about the lack of sobriety among the Bretons and Normans.

'If it weren't for them,' he muttered darkly, 'the law wouldn't have been changed. We wouldn't have lost the right to distil our own spirit.' French law was changed in 1960 and only proprietors existing then may keep the right to distil. Unfortunately this was just one year before Raymond and Claudette were married and took over the farm so the right will disappear with Grandpa when he dies, and the travelling still or *alambic* will no longer trundle into the courtyard to distil the fermenting barrels of plums and pears.

Lunch finally over we staggered outside to rest under the trees. Conversation languished for a while but soon the *boules* appeared and fierce games were played, English versus French, old versus young and town against country, with many a Gascon shout of rage or triumph as minute distances were checked with a ruler. Later some of us strolled through the farmyard to inspect the pigs, the rabbits, quail and guineafowl and on across the fields to admire the lake, newly dug for irrigation. In spite of government grants it was so expensive that the pump must wait for next year. In the next meadow a herd of Blondes d'Aquitaine regarded us inquisitively, flicking their creamy tails. We wandered back through grass alive with butterflies and grasshoppers and were about to make our farewells. Raymond looked surprised.

'But you can't go now. It's almost time for supper.' We were staggered. We had barely recovered from lunch. We tried to explain that we didn't think we could eat any more that day.

Claudette giggled. 'Wait and see. Now it's cooler. About nine o'clock you'll feel like a little something.'

It was with a certain sense of *déjà vu* that we once again assembled round the table. We were however one short. The taxidermist, accustomed it would appear only to stuffing other creatures, had gone home with a *crise de foie* but his wife was already seated, smiling and eager. 'How could I resist?' she appealed. 'I just left him tucked up in bed. He'll be all right.'

And so we began again, this time with a delicate beef *consommé* and, miraculously, our appetites returned. We drank no fine wines, just last year's local red, judiciously watered by all. But there were other treats, roasted guineafowl served on thin garlic rubbed toast was followed by a dish of *cèpes*, brown and crisp. Raymond closed his eyes as their perfume reached him.

'*Ah, ils poussent de bonnes choses dans les bois,*' he murmured. The *cèpes* were compared with *chanterelles, morilles, girolles* and a host of other fungi which they were amazed to learn are largely unappreciated in England.

'And you don't even collect *les trompettes de la mort?*'

We had to admit it. 'Are they good?' we asked.

'*Formidable!*' They sighed. There was no understanding the English. Raymond insisted that much of the tinned *pâté truffe* was actually flavoured with these *trompettes*, so named because they are black. We ate our *cèpes* dutifully but as they needed liberally flavouring with both garlic and parsley, I could not see that they were as delicious as a fresh field mushroom that needs nothing to improve it. After bowls of chocolate mousse and *crème anglaise* we were still talking and drinking coffee with Raymond who was as lively as at midday. We knew that he would be hard at work soon after six the following morning but we felt that we would take a little longer to recover.

Towards the end of the holiday Hugh Fowles, a colleague of Mike's, visited us en route to play in a tennis tournament in Bordeaux. A young and energetic craftsman, he helped us solve the problem of our corridor which, now the window was incorporated into our bedroom, was always dark unless the outer doors were left open. Unfortunately these were on the west side of the house which caught the prevailing wind. Each time the door between the corridor and the living room was opened, anyone standing in the kitchen corner, usually me, was almost blown away. Clearly what we needed were glazed inner doors but anything remotely modern would have been wrong.

Hugh and Mike went to see M. René who thought he might have a few old doors stacked in the derelict Boulangerie in the village. They finally unearthed a pair of glazed doors nine feet tall which were ideal. They built a frame with one door to be fixed and the other to be hinged open. The frame was huge and heavy and Hugh, who always reminds me of an El Greco figure, looked positively Christ-like as he edged it in on his shoulder. The frame was inched into place and the doors attached and now we can have the western light flooding in without the draught.

We did not get a great deal of work done on the house that summer. It was extremely hot – we had almost seven weeks of continuous sunshine – and also we were inundated, not with toads this year but with visitors. Visitors I have decided, give pleasure in every way; in the looking forward to their arrival, in the enjoyment of their company, and even in their eventual departure. Each group arrived hot, exhausted and often highly strung from the long journey and we watched the peace and the space begin to soothe them as it soothes us. Matthew brought a gorgeous blonde who slowly turned a pale burnished gold. Adam, by now working for his degree, came with Tom Harvey, a fellow student, and in one of their more energetic moments they built us a stone barbecue which, to everyone's surprise, still stands and works well. *Les Fostaires* returned, this time without mishap, and Tony too found yet another route to Bel-Air. Early one morning I counted eleven people quietly reading in various corners of the garden.

Although we were not in the mood for work it did not stop us planning. The new glass doors had improved the whole aspect of the west side of the house and we began to consider building a partly-covered terrace. It seemed the obvious use as it was an evening suntrap. Too hot in July, as August passed the halfway mark and the occasional breeze filtered down from the north, this protected spot became favourite for an evening drink. Of course it was still covered in weeds and the outer beam sloped wildly and was too low but the germ of the idea was sown. Even the old outhouse with the narrow wooden doors, which we used as a wood store and was home to a family of hedgehogs who snuffled nightly in and out, might be large enough to be converted to further accommodation. We were always considering the next task.

We were very happy with our new, enlarged bedroom except for the floor which, with a mixture of old and new cement, was an eyesore. Dark, quarry tiles would, we thought, be a mistake and we looked for something pale and neutral, and finally found them in a strange emporium in a field outside Fumel. It sold job lots of anything, including Spanish floortiles, which were so cheap that we bought enough to tile all the bedroom floors.

We saw our last visitors onto the train for Paris and as we stayed a few weeks longer that summer we were initiated into the most important harvest of the region, the plums.

'*On va ramasser les prunes la semaine prochaine,*' said Raymond, with a knowing smile. He knew that we were not involved in a major project at that moment. We had watched the trees grow heavier, the branches bending beneath the weight of the large, lavender-coloured plums. In each village and at every market the conversation was all concerned with *les prunes*.

'In Lot-et-Garonne over the next six weeks we shall harvest over ninety thousand *tonnes,*' said Raymond proudly. This special, local plum, called *la prune d'Ente* has a lavender bloom which rubs off to show the dark red skin beneath, accounting for its old name of *Robe Sergent*. Originally brought back to France by the Crusaders, most of its cultivation now takes place in this rolling countryside between the two rivers. The flesh is golden and very sweet, making it perfect for preserving by drying.

'Then they are called *les pruneaux*,' said Raymond.

'What we call prunes,' we told him.

He laughed. '*Que c'est compliqué.*'

Harvesting plums filled each September. Before the *Coopérative* was built to buy the plums and dry them by gas in great quantities, each farm had its own wood-fired oven or *étuve*. The one on Raymond's farm was built in 1928 to replace a much earlier one. 'But you have one up at Bel-Air,' he said. Of course, we had forgotten. The small out-house where the hedgehogs lived in the wood-pile, Raymond had always called that *l'étuve*. We now saw that the sloping roof had an inner flat roof of smoke-blackened terracotta tiles; a crude tin chimney protruded from the end wall. Now the curiously narrow doors were explained. It was through these that the plum-laden trolley would have been pushed.

Down on the farm Grandpa had been pottering about for days tidying up the year's accumulation in front of the doors of their *étuve*. 'This year is the last time I'll do it,' he declared, 'It's too much work.' He lights the oven every year to cook a few hundred kilos of plums, especially the half cooked or *mi-cuit* which will be preserved in *eau-de-vie*, but once it is alight he must get up twice a night to replenish the wood.

Next day his old comrade from his time as a prisoner of war arrived to help him. They reminisced as they mended broken trays and oiled the wheels of *le wagonet*, a long, iron trolley which has eight shelves for the trays and holds over 300 kilos of plums. He showed us how he would push it on the rails through the high wooden doors into *l'étuve* where thick iron pipes line the walls and carry the heat from the fire pit next door.

We greeted each other in the early morning sunlight. Fernande was there, stolid and smiling in flowered hat and apron, also Grandma and Claudette, barefoot M. Demoli unusually prompt, M. René's sister and a friend, Philippe and Véronique and two cousins from Agen. The women chatted as we collected our green plastic baskets, familiar from the potato harvest, and strolled down to the orchard where Raymond waited, a small iron ladder propped against the first tree. The first day of the harvest was clearly an occasion, and he was doubly pleased to begin by initiating us.

'*Eh alors,*' he said with a grin. He shinned up the ladder and shook each branch with his strong brown arms. A cascade of lavender plums covered the carefully raked earth and we bent to pick them up. Before we had finished he moved on and shook the next tree, and so it continued. We tipped our full baskets into crates which were placed in rows to make them easier for collection later with the trailer. It was not hard work to begin with and unlike potatoes you could eat as many as you liked, but as the morning wore on the aching began. I watched Fernande, easily the strongest and quickest worker. Thick legs astride, she never bent her knees but would occasionally rest one forearm against her thigh to relieve her back.

Raymond delighted in tricking her. It was clearly a ritual appreciated by all, even Fernande herself. High in the tree hidden by the thick branches he would call her, '*Eh Fernande!*' Innocent and glad of a chance to straighten she would gaze upward shading her eyes. A quick shake and down rained the plums. She never minded the laughter but she never remembered either. He caught her every time.

The dogs chased imaginary rabbits and each other. The women gossiped and, as usual, exchanged recipes; *poule au pot, alouettes sans têtes,* which turned out to be beef-olives, and compared the various sauces in which to cook them. The recipes went on and on as we slowly moved up the rows of trees. Cardigans and pullovers hung abandoned on the branches as the sun rose higher and wasps buzzed round the baskets. Our hands were stained and sticky and the smell of ripe fruit was almost overpowering. At last all fifty crates were full and Mike drove slowly between the trees while Raymond and M. Demoli swung them up onto the trailer.

It was midday and everyone straightened gratefully, groaning and stretching. '*Maintenant,*' said Grandma, '*on peut redresser les reins.*' I really did feel as though my kidneys had floated up somewhere between my shoulder blades. We left the plums to the wasps and trailed back to the farm and into the cool kitchen. There was a pleasurable jostling

at the sink to clean our sugary fingers before a welcome
apéritif.

In the forty minutes or so since Claudette had left us she
had managed to prepare a meal for fourteen. We sat down
to sorrel soup, melon, home-cured ham, macaroni cheese
and grilled steak followed by tomato and onion salad and
finally for desert, pears from the orchard. We were
ravenous. There had been as usual no mid-morning
anything. Each of us was concerned with replenishing
energy for the afternoon.

By two-thirty we were en route to the next orchard about
a mile away. Matthew and I bumped slowly along sitting
on the high mudguard of the old tractor with Grandpa
behind us in his battered old 2CV van. Fernande whirred
past us on her mobylette and M. René's sister and her
friend, still exchanging recipes no doubt, had managed to
cram themselves into M. Demoli's disreputable car between
all the scrap metal.

M. Demoli took on the job of shaking the trees in the
afternoon. Half hidden in the leaves he braced himself and
sent down the plums. With his wild, gleaming eyes and
wheezy shouts one looked again to make sure that those
bare black feet were not in fact cloven hooves. In the days
that followed the smell of wood smoke and cooking plums
filled the air for miles. The bulk of the harvest was taken
to the *Coopérative* and there were races each evening to be
the first tractor and trailer on the road to Monflanquin.

Grandpa was constantly busy, filling the large flat trays
or *claies*, loading them into the *wagonet* after washing them
and pushing the filled *wagonet* in and out of *l'étuve*. Were
they cooked enough? Perhaps a little longer. They normally
cooked very slowly for twenty-four hours. I began to learn
the language of the prunes. The smallest, hardly worth the
drying, were *les fretins*. Grandpa called the largest *les
impériales*. *Le triage*, the grading of the dried fruit, was done
by Grandma and her friend, Antoinette. Antoinette was part
of *le système*. She had once lived in the village but was now
looked after by her daughter and son-in-law in Paris. Each

September she returned *pour les prunes* and the two old friends sat hour after hour sorting the still warm glistening fruit as they talked inevitably about *autrefois*.

Claudette was busy preparing the jars for preserving *les impériales* in *eau-de-vie* which had been distilled the previous year. First she packed the still warm prunes into the jars and stood them on the hot step in front of the oven. She then prepared the syrup, 300 grammes of sugar dissolved in one litre of *eau-de-vie* for each two litre jar of plums. She stirred it very carefully as obviously it could easily catch fire. The syrup was poured gently over the warm fruit and the jars sealed immediately. 'They are best left for two years,' she said. 'After five years they begin to disintegrate but we never manage to keep them that long.' I could understand why.

The smallest and any damaged plums were collected in large barrels. These were covered and left to ferment for at least a month before being distilled into the *eau-de-vie* for the following year. Everywhere one looked *les prunes* and *les pruneaux* were the centre of attention.

The night before we left, after eating with the family which had by now become a welcome ritual after a day spent packing up the house, we sat nibbling more prunes. 'Why don't the English buy more of our prunes?' we were asked. It was difficult to try to explain their school dinner image and their lack of chic, in this region which dedicates a month every year to this purple harvest and even writes poems to *la prune*. 'How do they prefer them, the English?' they enquired, thinking of their own *noix de veau aux pruneaux* or *terrine de lapin Gascon*, the rabbit flesh laced with prunes.

'Mostly stewed with custard,' we admitted. They shook their heads.

Who knows? Perhaps we might be tempted by the advice of the Duc de Guise who in 1588, it is said, after arduous nights spent with Madame de Noirmoutiers ate prunes in the morning as a restorative from *les fatigues de l'amour*. Next morning as we left Claudette presented us with a jar to keep us all going through the coming winter.

11

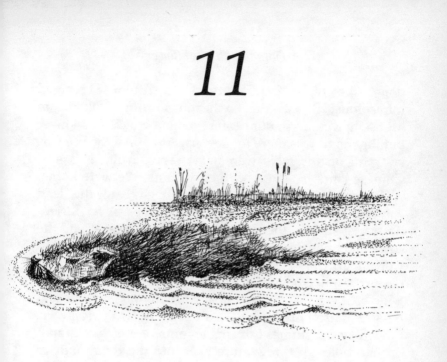

*B*efore we left that summer we had talked about planting some more trees. So far we had a greengage and an apricot, which Raymond had planted for us when we first came, on the far edge of the field. On the south side of the house were two small pines and what had originally been two sumachs, planted by Grandma, which had now become five. I had put in two blue *cupressus* and a *thuya orientalis* to protect us from the westerlies but I now hankered for something more exotic. One of those dark, slender Mediterranean cypresses to grow into a tall exclamation mark by the house, or an *Acacia Albezzia* with its wonderful fluffy pink blossom, perhaps a Judas tree to give us colour in the spring; we discussed it with Grandpa.

'It's the wrong time to plant trees,' he cried. 'Trees should be planted at the feast of Saint Catherine. *À la Sainte Catherine toute branche prend racine!*' And when would that be? At the end of November.

That was all the excuse we needed to fly down for ten days. After all those six hundred mile drives that we had done, the flight from Gatwick to Toulouse seemed miraculous. It was the connections from Toulouse to Monsempron-Libos, our nearest station, which took longer but Raymond was there to meet us. At Bel-Air the fire was laid and on the table were wine, eggs, fruit, a vase of Chinese lanterns and a bowl of walnuts. We were home.

Our two great ash trees were strangely bare, the dead leaves in the drive blown into musty heaps. A few dried-up scarlet shreds still clung to the virginia creeper and the cows had gone down to their winter quarters but the days were mild, the air so clean after London that it seemed perfumed and wonderfully shaped clouds bowled across the wide blue sky. We burned heavy logs in our *cheminée* and bought an iron fire-back with a design of two *vendangeurs* in medieval costumes carrying an outsize bunch of grapes on two poles. It threw more heat into the room and we cooked sausages and chops on a trivet over the hot ashes.

Everyone seemed surprised and pleased to see us. I think they almost associate us with the swallows and we were out of season. They looked different in their felt caps, thick stockings and fleecy lined slippers – very necessary with cold, tiled floors. The markets were full of woollen socks and underclothes, hunting coats with rows of pockets, cartridge belts, fancy saddles and riding crops, hazelnuts, walnuts and pumpkins. In the covered market where the farmers' wives sell their produce there were already rows of plump golden corpses – the specially fattened ducks and geese for making *confit* and *foie gras*. Smart town ladies prodded them with manicured fingers while the red-cheeked, aproned sellers extolled their birds and the quality of the maize on which they had been fed. It was interesting to be there at such a different time of year.

One morning a notice went up in the village shop,
   GRAND LOTTO SAMEDI SOIR A NEUF HEURES.
'You will come, won't you?' asked Mme Laval who runs the shop, the café and the petrol pump. Before we could reply Mme Barrou arrived on her Solex to collect her bread – the largest loaf in the shop.

'Vous allez venir, vous deux?' she demanded. When I learned that Lotto was in fact Bingo I was not over eager but when they told us that all the proceeds were to support the village school it seemed churlish to refuse and, I thought, I could still do with improving my numbers in French. *'Il faut y aller de bonne heure pour avoir des places,'* yelled Mme Barrou as she revved up her Solex and wobbled off, the loaf tied to the back. Everyone in the shop agreed, eyes bright at the coming excitement. Mike groaned but we obviously had to go.

We arrived early. However by half-past nine, as the outdoor faces that usually smiled at us from a tractor were still crowding into the room, we realised that the start would depend on how long each took to greet the other.

'Bonsoir.'

'Bonsoir.'

'Ça va?'

'Ça va.' Many of them must have seen each other twice already that day. Kiss, kiss and yet another for luck.

'How warm it is for the time of the year.'

'And the ground so wet, *Pardi!'*

With smiles and shrugs they passed on to the next neighbour and it all began again.

We bought our cards for the evening at 25 francs for four. They were very dog-eared and, judging by the rubber stamp in the corner, had been borrowed from the next commune. Along the length of the tables, like harvest festival, were small heaps of maize grains with which to cover the numbers as they were called. Mme Laval's husband, who besides helping his wife is also a busy farmer, blew into the microphone. His mischievous grandson Julien eyed the large drum of numbered plastic balls and was swiftly removed by Madame.

'Alors,' he began. His voice boomed out and he stopped, cleared his throat and smiled nervously at the eager faces before him. *'Mesdames, messieurs. Il faut commencer.'* As we all settled down he announced the first prizes for the evening.

'*Pour la première ligne . . . Un poulet, deux bouteilles de vin. La carte complète . . . Un jambon.*'

The hall was hushed as the first game began. After the first few games were finished we watched the delighted winners stowing away *rôtis* of veal and pork, jars of *confit de canard* and the famous prunes in *eau-de-vie* and we began to understand just why local bingo was an event not to be missed. When each prize was edible it was a serious affair.

Raymond and Claudette kept an eye on our cards as well as their own and we were slightly ashamed to find ourselves checking each other's numbers in English, especially those over seventy. We consoled ourselves with the fact that the caller would insist on shouting the occasional number in patois to cries of protest from the youngsters but to the obvious delight of the older generation.

At ten-thirty it was time for the *entracte*. In this the region of the *Vieux Cahors*, where the arrival of the Beaujolais Nouveau creates hardly a ripple, they all confined themselves to Orangina or Le Schweppes, but how they ate! Huge platefuls of *beignets*, a local doughnut, and rolled up *crèpes* arrived and vanished. The children played beneath the tunnels of the long tables and the room reverberated with loud, happy voices.

'*Alors.*' Eyes down again. The prizes varied. Two pheasants, a turkey and, for the whole card, a *tourtière*. We now understood that most of the presents had been donated. There were only fourteen pupils in the school but it clearly had the support of the entire village.

There was an extra excitement when a surprise lot was announced. Claudette won and it was revealed to be a pair of wild ducks. She stood up proudly to display them, their wings flapping, the male with his glistening green head and his drab consort. Delighted, she returned them gently to their box, soothing their ruffled feathers with a practised hand. What fun it was!

At long last the final game and the prize for which they had all been waiting.

'*Une cuisse de boeuf,*' yelled M. Laval, his voice husky and the sweat running down into his eyebrows. His assistant heaved up the prize and the whole room, as one, gazed at the eighteen kilos of prime beef. They drooled, eighteen kilos of the best *bifteck*, grilled with garlic, naturally, perhaps with shallots, braised over vine twigs, *en daube* with *pruneaux* or *cèpes*, those highly prized white fleshed edible toadstools which are so popular in this region. While passionate discussions of favourite recipes exploded about the room the weary caller pleaded for attention. It was past midnight and many of the children were asleep, tousled heads among the doughnut crumbs. At last the noise subsided as they realised that the coveted prize had yet to be won.

In the rolling accent of the south-west M. Laval made a final effort. '*Cinquante et un. Trente-quatre. Trois.*' The tension mounted as we glanced sideways at each other's cards. Only one more needed over there and there too. '*Trente-sept. Quatorze,*' he intoned. Sturdy, roughened hands were poised over the cards, the grain of maize squeezed tightly between finger and thumb. '*Soixante-cinque.*' A great shout went up, followed immediately by the sighs and groans of the losers, and a young father of five was on his feet, supported by his delirious family, his round face flushed with triumph.

I suppose they might have come if the prizes had been mere cash but it wouldn't have been half the fun. The winners packed their spoils carefully into cartons and the children were throwing handfuls of maize at each other as we reeled out into the dark and starry night.

We planted our trees; an *Acacia Albezia*, a weeping willow and a dark green Mediterranean cypress but alas, by the following year only the cypress remained. So much for Saint Catherine!

Next Easter was early and cold. True, the fields were full of daffodils and narcissus, but they shivered and shook in the bitter north wind. It whistled down through the break in the distant woods, straight under our porch and in through every gap round the front door. Now we knew why

Anaïs had planted a high hazel hedge which we had thoughtlessly uprooted.

Friends came from Scotland and found it as cold as Aboyne and without the comforts of carpets and central heating. We bought thick socks in the market and found that the best way to get warm was to saw up logs for the fire. Our friends, generous as ever, had brought many small delicacies and we had fun planning a Scottish menu to entertain the Bertrands. We built a huge fire, hung a blanket across the door to keep out the draughts and warmed ourselves with Cock-a-leekie soup, Arbroath smokies, haggis, and roast venison. Claudette, as always, found every dish intriguing and Grandpa, who loves fish, was delighted with the smokies. Of course no sooner had our friends flown home than the wind died away and the spring really arrived. In spite of the distractions of long walks through cowslip-lined lanes we disciplined ourselves sufficiently to tile our bedroom floor and were extremely pleased with the result.

On Thursday mornings we almost always go to market. The only decision we must make is which one to go to. Our local town of Monflanquin has had a Thursday morning market since 1256. The one at Libos, some ten kilometres distant, is not quite so old but is much larger, the whole town centre being closed to traffic and some hundred stalls being ready for business before eight o'clock. It is a cornucopia of seasonal fruit and flowers, vegetables, gleaming fish straight from Bordeaux, piles of exotic mushrooms, hundreds of cheeses, every variety of honey, spices, nuts, and olives; paella cooking on the spot in a massive pan, sizzling doughnuts, cures for rheumatism and lethal knives labelled *saigne lapin*.

One morning I noticed an unusual sight. Past the homemade goats' cheese and the lady who sells quails' eggs, at the very end of the market, stood a large, swarthy woman, the table before her heaped with a jumble of old clothes. Local ladies eyed her sideways and hurried by.

Farmers' wives carrying boxes of chicks stared uncomprehendingly at the crumpled pile. I looked at her crudely drawn notice.

TOUT A 5 FRANCS

I have always had a passion for secondhand clothes. To me they are like theatrical costumes. Someone else chose them, wore them and then discarded them. Who? What were they like? At 50p a garment how could I resist? The stall holder smiled revealing several gold teeth and with a large brown hand she turned the clothes and I heard for the first time the expression *'Fouillez Madame, fouillez.'* That was it. I was hooked.

To begin with they were not, of course, English clothes. There were unfamiliar styles and fabrics with French, Dutch, German and occasionally Italian labels. In minutes I had found an Indian red velour skirt the exact shade of a favourite jacket brought in a sale at 'Bus Stop' years before. It was fully lined with the zip going right up the waistband as with most French skirts. I could hardly wait to get it home. Would it fit? It did, Perfectly.

I washed it and wore it a few days later. Claudette admired it. *'Pas mauvais,'* I agreed, *'pour cinq francs.'* She shook her head and laughingly corrected me. Would Ruth never get her numbers right?

'Non. non. non!' she cried *'Cent francs.'*

I persisted, *'Cinq francs.'* I held up five fingers and her jaw dropped.

'C'est vrai? Mais . . . òu?' And that was how I learned what secondhand clothes are called in France; *la friperie*. What a wonderfully frivolous name!

Since that day the trade in secondhand clothing has grown rapidly. There are ever more stalls and *la friperie* has become a harmless addiction. Claudette sometimes comes with me to the largest which is held every other Tuesday in the exquisite town of Villeneuve-sur-Lot. As early as we can, like a couple of conspirators, we hurtle down the leafy lanes to market. The normal buying of provisions over, and the car loaded, we are then free to indulge our *fantaisie*. Free to hurry down past the war memorial where St George is permanently slaying the dragon, to the far end of the wide, flower-decked boulevard. There the coloured umbrellas ripple in the morning breeze and the twenty or so stalls are in full swing, many of them run by Algerians. Some *entrepreneurs* have vans going twice a week to Holland where the clothes, collected from all over Europe, are cleaned, baled and sold by weight. The turnover is rapid. The days when ladies looked askance at secondhand clothes are long since gone, and many French women are keen to clothe themselves and their families for a tenth of the normally high prices.

It is the system of pricing that helps make *la friperie* such fun. There is very little grading according to quality so that, for example, all the skirts on a stall will be marked 30 francs but they will range from a garish horror in multi-coloured crimplene to a fine, wool-georgette silk-lined model with a Swiss label. Some stall holders don't even separate the garments. Everything is in a great heap and it is there that the best bargains can sometimes be found. I bought an elegant shirtwaister, unsure until I checked in a German dictionary that it was 75% raw silk. It washes like a dream and cost me a pound. All you need to learn are sizes and fabric names in French, Italian and German, and it helps to carry a tape measure in case the labels are missing.

With prices like these you can take a chance on the most outlandish garments, and if they don't fit tear them up. They are cheaper than dusters and much more fun. All our visitors indulge and on our return from market, after we have unloaded the wonderful selection of seasonal delights that make shopping here such a joy, we always finish with a fashion parade from *la friperie*.

When Adam brought Cas, my daughter-in-love, for the first time she came back with six carrier bags crammed with clothes. He watched her pirouetting past him in a succession of garments, an olive-green jump suit, an outsize red and white striped shirt, a blue velour dressing gown with a hood, and a duster coat in black moiré taffeta. 'The coat

alone would have cost me a fortune in King's Road Chelsea,'
she crowed. Adam grew paler by the minute. They were
on a tight budget. Eventually, the parade finished, she
picked up the clothes and headed for the washing machine,
calling triumphantly over her shoulder. 'Relax! *Tout pour*
fifteen quid!' The best bargain I have bought so far is an
apparently unworn almond green cashmere sweater for a
pound. But of course there's always the next *friperie*.

That summer, when we first arrived, we were surprised to
see, hanging on a wire at the entrance to our track a row
of furry pelts. Too large to be moles, we wondered what
they were. Not for long, our village was agog with the great
plague of *ragondins*. As they were described they grew larger
and fiercer. What could they be? Philippe fetched the
dictionary; coypu. None of us had ever seen one. Were they
dangerous? No, well at least they thought not. They were
reluctant to spoil the drama entirely. Then what exactly was
the problem?

Grandpa explained that the *ragondins* were destroying the
ponds and lakes by making huge nesting holes in the banks
which allowed the water to escape. Now we understood
the general consternation. Water for both crops and animals
is at a premium during the long hot summers. As in
England, coypu had once been farmed for their fur, nutria,
which had been popular. But to have perfect pelts they
demanded a great deal of feeding and as the fur became
increasingly out of fashion the farmers of Savoy simply
released them. '*Et maintenant ils viennent dans notre Sud-
Ouest*,' everyone complained bitterly.

Each day new sightings were reported. At this farm and
that another one had been shot, another had got away. They
bred faster than rabbits, we were told. One morning we
were down at the farm when Grandpa returned triumphant.
'*Venez voir*,' he shouted. There, laid out in the courtyard
for all to see was a dead *ragondin*. Large as a well-fed cat,
with two huge bright orange front teeth which protruded
over its lower jaw, it was not an attractive sight. And such

a thick strong rat-like tail! A small crowd gathered, neighbouring children arrived on bicycles and inevitably someone enquired whether or not it was edible. Grandpa shook his head. '*Ce n'est qu'un gros rat,*' he said, picking it up by its tail and looking pleased with himself. The children shrieked and backed away.

The weather became hotter. The maize in *le grand champ* grew, it seemed, by inches every day. Raymond looked at it anxiously. 'If the *ragondin* gets in there she'll do a lot of damage,' he muttered.

'Do they eat maize?' we asked. '*Bien sûr!*' By this time they were rumoured to eat almost everything. One morning M. Girot, our other neighbour through whose farm we had so carelessly driven on the day we had found Bel-Air, stopped his tractor outside the house. Apart from Raymond, he and his sons are the only people who ever drive past.

'*Bonjour.*'

'*Bonjour.*'

'*Ça va?*' '*Ça va.*'

'*Vous avez vu?*'

'*Quoi?*'

'*Le ragondin!*'

There was one in our pond he declared. Had he seen it? No, but he'd seen the tracks. We went to look. Sure enough, his farmer's eyes had noticed the round tunnels through the long thick grass. 'There and there, look!' he said. It was undeniable. What to do? '*Il faut le tuer,*' he said simply and got back onto his tractor.

The pond is about a hundred yards from the house. That evening as we sat watching from the garden a large ripple disturbed the water. Through binoculars we saw her clearly. Why *her* I do not know. The great teeth were still curious and repulsive but in the water she was graceful and a joy to watch. As she dived to pull up the weeds with those specially designed teeth the strong thick tail lashed up to balance her. Not as sleek as an otter she nevertheless had her own appeal and we were loth to destroy her. We took to creeping along to the pond and sometimes we got close enough to see her slide into the water from the far bank.

The next Sunday we were to entertain *toute la famille* for lunch. I was busy preparing a menu, searching for extra dishes to amuse and intrigue them. This time it was Scotch eggs, which they had never seen before, and slices of pear stuffed with Roquefort and sprinkled with poppy seeds. I had intended to try this the previous holiday but had discovered that edible poppy seeds were unheard of here. I remember the smart grocer in Villeneuve looking astonished at such a request and suggesting that I might find them in the *Agrilot* where they do indeed sell seeds, but for planting, not cooking.

It was another very hot day. The family arrived, as usual, dead on twelve-thirty. Claudette brought a huge bowl of strawberries which she had just picked and Raymond a bottle of his own dessert wine to drink with them. Grandpa however, when he appeared, chugging up the track with Grandma in their 2CV, brought a shotgun and handed it to Mike. 'C'est pour le ragondin,' he roared. Mike took the gun and did not answer. 'Otherwise I shall set traps,' said the old man, taking his usual place at the head of the table.

The thought of that beautiful, sleek body helpless and bleeding in a trap was out of the question as well he knew, and about three-thirty, when we had finished eating, Mike took the gun. He and Raymond went to sit on a grassy bank near the pond. In a post prandial stupor it was difficult to concentrate on the dark water. Patterned by fierce sunlight filtering through overhanging branches, it was alive with dragonflies and water boatmen. A movement caught Mike's eye and, turning, he saw *le ragondin* running down the field towards the pond. He nudged Raymond who had by now actually dozed off. 'Elle est là.' he whispered.

Raymond shook himself awake. 'Tire, tire,' he hissed urgently. aiming slightly ahead of the running animal, Mike fired. To his astonishment she stopped, rolled over, quivered and was still. Mike's sadness was eased by having killed her outright with one shot. His reputation as a marksman was high in the village but our *ragondin* was no more.

There was an abundance of greengages that summer. Claudette, Fernande, Grandma and I sat in the shade under the hangar cutting up fruit for jam until our thumbs were sore. Fernande and Claudette went to pick pears and Grandma to cut lettuces for supper and I was left to watch the jam. The frothy mixture seethed gently in a great copper pan on a large iron trivet. The outsize gas ring flickered and flared. When, from time to time, I stirred the jam with a metre-long black wooden baton, which had apparently belonged to Grandpa's mother, it bubbled fiercely. Everything was so extra large that I felt like a character in the giant's kitchen in 'Jack and the Beanstalk'. Satisfied that it was not burning, I lay the baton across the pan and lazily watched a narrow band of sweet scum like an encrusted bracelet, dry a few inches from the end. As the scented steam rose, the cooing of the turtle-dove in her cage merged with the gentle bubbling of the jam. Two flies crawled across the table. The dog looked up, stretched his front legs, yawned and went back to sleep.

I wondered whether Anaïs had sat like this up at Bel-Air stirring the jam. Perhaps she had left Alaïs to mind it while she went to cut the lettuces. From the *rente viagère* contract that Raymond had shown me I now knew that she had been born in 1871 in a village some ten miles away but that her husband Justin, the eldest of three sons, was born at Bel-Air in 1866. When the youngest boy was barely five years old their mother had died leaving their father, one *Sieur Pierre Costes*, to bring up the three children. He was described as an *'ancien tisserand'*, and I wondered if those crude and worm-eaten tools for the teasing out of wool that we had found in the attic, had once belonged to him.

In the hat-box, the contents of which were becoming ever more fascinating, were some fragile letters in an elegant, spidery hand, addressed to M. Costes and dated February and May 1876. They suggest that his wife may have already been in poor health. The first letter is in reply to M. Costes's request for a consultation by letter from *la somnambulla* – an old word for a clairvoyant. This, it is explained, is not possible because she does not give written advice for fear of being brought before a tribunal. The writer, a cousin living in Bordeaux, suggests that M. Costes should write again, enclosing a lock of hair which he will take personally to her. In the second letter he writes in detail of the visit and lists the prescribed treatment.

1) One tablet of *blancard* each morning and two at night.

2) A tisane made from the roots of wild strawberry and linseed to be taken half an hour after the tablets.

3) A demi-enema every day for fifteen days.

A diet of good meat stock, made from undercooked mutton or beef, and vintage wine to drink – 'because she has need of blood'. On the 22nd of May he writes again asking his cousin for a progress report. He warns him against using any other treatment and says he will warn him when another lock of hair is needed, the present one sufficing for a second consultation. He ends his most concerned letter, *'Recevez les salutations de celui qui reste votre ami pour la vie.'* If the remedy was for Justin's mother it does not seem to have helped for she died three years later.

Anaïs was eighteen when, in 1889, she and Justin were married. Old Sieur Pierre Costes then made over the property to the young couple but retained the life interest and the revenue, Justin working the land. The farm was much smaller and with many debts outstanding and so Anaïs continued in service. I have been told that at one time she worked in a large house which is just visible on the brow of the hill. Did she look down and wish that Bel-Air was really hers, I wonder. Alaïs was born three years later. Did she take him with her to work or leave him for the old man to look after, and how old was he when he caught polio? No one can tell me.

Although handicapped, Alaïs was able to work. In her account book for 1910 his mother proudly records her eighteen-year-old son giving her 50 francs. She seems to have spent it all on him buying three shirts, a jacket and trousers and a pair of *brodequins*, a kind of lace-up boot. Old Sieur Pierre Costes lived on until 1912 when Justin paid 800 francs to each of his brothers and at last, he and Anaïs were master and mistress of Bel-Air. It was then that they had the little house enlarged, building on the differently roofed section with its two bedrooms below and extended attic above. They must have made many plans together, long-term plans as farmers must do, but within two years the horror of the Great War would overturn them all. Alaïs, handicapped though he was, would be drafted into the reserve and, the cruellest irony of all, Justin, spared the battle would, in 1918, die of a heart attack.

12

On Sundays, if we are not eating chez Bertrand or they with us, we like to go some ten kilometres away to the village of Lacapelle Biron. On the borders of Lot-et-Garonne, it was created almost by accident by a long forgotten Marquis of the nearby château of Biron. Suffering from both asthma and gout, this unfortunate nobleman could not bear the noisy market which was held each Monday beneath his walls. 'Send them somewhere else,' he wheezed and so, taking their name with them, the traders of Biron moved down the hill and across the fields to the ancient hamlet of Lacapelle. The two names joined together, the village flourished and Monday is still market day.

It is essential to book at the Restaurant Palissy which is named after Bernard Palissy, renaissance potter, scientist and philosopher. Born of humble parents in the next village of St Avit, he spent years researching his glazes, becoming so impoverished that he was reduced to burning his furniture and floorboards to fire his kiln. For Catherine de Medici he built a grotto in her Tuileries Gardens, decorating it with enamelled lizards, toads and serpents. He travelled widely and wrote on a wide range of subjects but always begged his students not to listen to those scientists who sat all day propounding theories. Always a craftsman he wrote 'with all the theory in the world you can make nothing, not even a shoe. Practice must engender theory.' He became a Huguenot and eventually Royal patronage could protect him no longer. He was imprisoned in the Bastille where, at the age of eighty-one, he died. There is a statue of him in Villeneuve-sur-Lot, a gentle, scholarly figure holding one of his famous dishes, a tiny creature curled up inside.

Outside the restaurant which bears his name the tables are always crowded with customers taking their aperitifs. 'We have laid a hundred and seventy places today,' announces M. Allo, the head waiter, as he greets us. Teeth flashing, M. Allo plays his role as though Feydeau himself had written it, glorying in every detail. Perhaps it is because he is really the local postman and only has two performances at the weekend. Otherwise he must tear across the countryside in his yellow van. Today all that is forgotten. Resplendent in a dazzling white, starched jacket, head to one side, he whirls and weaves between the tables at ever increasing speed. '*J'arrive. J'arrive!*' he calls, sweat already trickling down his florid face. He loves every moment.

The menu hardly ever varies but I suspect there would be an outcry if it did. This is what we come for, the *jambon du pays*, the *écrevisses*, the *ris de veau*. Restaurant Palissy is respected by local families and it is they who eat there in the winter when the tourists are far away. The dining room fills quickly. Many of the customers know each other and there is a lot of kissing. Most of the families are of three generations, all stylishly dressed, even though most of them will be at work in the fields tomorrow. Trays of melons, already on the table, perfume the room which reverberates with serious debate as menus are studied. The most expensive with seven courses will not cost more than twelve pounds and you can eat extremely well for seven. There is a choice for each course but no pressure to decide. Lunch will go on until four o'clock. Friends wave as the last stragglers take their places in the crowded room. *Bon appetit!*

Our soup is a tasty *consommé* in which float tiny beads of sago called, more poetically in France, *perles du Japon*. After the soup we sample the house wine, a *vin ordinaire* in name only, for the local Cahors is good. The melons are perfect; grown locally, they can be harvested at precisely the right moment. One of our party, not liking seafood, has chosen a cheaper menu. Her thin slices of home-cured ham hang over the edge of the plate. 'Don't worry,' we urge, 'you have plenty of time.' And we begin to demolish our mountain of langoustines, mussels, clams, winkles, prawns, shrimps and cockles in their shells.

M. Allo speeds past, balancing three trays piled with debris. He works twice as fast as the waitresses, all half his age, apart from his wife who is short, plump and calm, and smilingly approves his performance from across the room. '*Eh voilà!*' he beams and with a flourish presents the *écrevisses*, bright coral red, succulent and gleaming, sprinkled with chopped garlic and parsley and flambéed in Armagnac.

The first time we tasted *écrevisses* was chez Bertrand. Early one morning Grandpa had taken Mike and Matthew to his secret spot on a nearby stream. They had baited a line of square muslin nets with his special bait, chunks of pork fat dipped in Pernod. When the nets were slowly raised after a short wait the black shiny *écrevisses* were clinging to the underside, trying to reach the bait. 'When I was a boy,' grumbled the old man, 'there were scores in this stream. Nowadays . . .' he shrugged, throwing his hands in the air.

In the event they caught a mere half dozen and the following day at Sunday lunch, after the first three courses, Claudette solemnly presented them in the centre of a large plate. 'How are we going to divide them?' she asked. 'I suppose those who caught them should have first choice.' She put one onto each plate and then went back into the kitchen laughing, appearing again with a heaped bowl of *écrevisses* which she had generously bought at market.

Now, as then, we are surrounded by sounds of sucking and crunching and sighs of pleasure. Bread is dipped in the sauce and fingers finally licked before being almost reluctantly wiped on the scented tissues provided.

One of us had the *ris-de-veau*. 'How were they?' we enquire. 'Wonderful,' she sighs, 'have a taste.' The sweetbreads are in a delicate sauce with olives and tiny mushrooms and they melt in the mouth. At every other table sampling of each others' dishes is going on. This is what Le Palissy is all about. Greasy-chinned faces beam at each other and M. Allo beams at everyone.

With our *rôti de veau* and *confit de poulet* we drink an older wine but still a Cahors. More sampling follows. We decide that the chicken has been preserved in goose fat, delicious! M. Allo brings a fresh green salad and then the cheese board which is small but interesting, a *bleu des Causses* from the stony hillside to the east, a fresh goat cheese and a Pyrenée.

Dessert is a choice of ice creams, chocolate, sorbet of lemon or blackcurrant, *vacherin* – vanilla with slices of prune inside, or a slice of *tourtière*. As he finally brings our coffee M. Allo is anxious to know if we have enjoyed our meal. We assure him it was wonderful. He beams. We have a favour to ask. May we take his photograph? His jaw drops. He stares at us blankly then rushes from the room. Have we offended him? He returns at a run frantically combing his hair, and poses. His great shoulders heave as he tries to suppress a sudden fit of giggles. In an effort to be serious he clasps his hands tightly. Click, it is done. He rushes off again to return moments later with a baked Alaska. It is a special treat for someone's birthday and with a flourish he lights the sparklers stuck in the top. As we leave Le Palissy customers still left are singing Happy Birthday, M. Allo as loudly as all the others.

Outside the heat bounces off the pale stone houses. We narrow our eyes and search for sunglasses. We cross the square and pause as each well-fed customer will on emerging into the sunlight to face the unique monument in the centre. It gained for its sculptor, Buisseret, the Grand Prix de Rome in 1947. One cannot fail to be moved by the simplicity and eloquence of the line of arms which rises so starkly from the earth. The hands hold a massive stone slab which bears the names of those who never returned to their beloved *Sud-Ouest*.

The old people need no monument to remind them of that other Sunday morning. A Sunday morning in May 1944 when, just after dawn, a battalion of the SS Das Reich under General Lamerdine, infamous for ordering the total destruction of Oradour sur Glane, encircled the village. The Resistance were active in the surrounding wooded hills and as a reprisal all the men of Lacapelle Biron were rounded up and taken to a derelict paper mill further up the valley. As the day wore on, other men arriving to visit relatives were also seized. A father hearing that his son was held went to protest. The Germans took him too. By the evening the hostages numbered forty-seven. They were transported to Auschwitz where more than half of them died. The monument marks the spot from which the trucks left.

The crickets are singing as we walk slowly to our car parked under a tree. Is it perhaps the knowledge that life can never be taken for granted that makes these sturdy people enjoy their work and their leisure with such intensity?

The sun grew fiercer each day. By the end of the following week *une canicule*, a heatwave, was officially announced. Under our north-facing porch, which had funnelled the bitter wind at Easter, it was still 92 degrees long after the sun had disappeared, flaring the horizon with streaks of fire. Adam and Cas were due to leave the following day and we had been invited to spend their last evening with friends some twenty miles away. Later, on leaving for home at about eleven, a few spots of rain began to fall and thinking of our parched garden, we were glad. However, within a few miles our windscreen wipers were unable to cope with torrential rain and we were forced to stop.

We drank coffee at a bar and waited for the rain to ease. The tree-lined roads were winding and difficult to negotiate. When we were able to start again it was with relief that we eventually neared home and familiar territory but it was never to be quite the same again.

Since the great storm in London in October 1987 what happened that night in our little part of France becomes perhaps insignificant, but at that time I had never experienced anything like it. Adam, having already got out of the car two or three times to move fallen branches climbed out yet again as our headlights picked out another obstacle. A whole tree blocked the road. We turned to try to get home from another direction, splashed along the muddy, debris-strewn lane and eventually, with relief, climbed our own winding track up to the house.

'Never mind,' I shouted as I raced to get under the porch and unlock the door, 'we'll soon be warm and dry.' I reached for the light switch. Nothing. I did not need a light to tell me something was wrong. I could hear the water dripping inside the house. Once inside a torch revealed a dark hole in the ceiling, and we splashed across the floor to our bedroom to see our saturated bed standing in several inches of dirty water.

Mercifully, Adam and Cas's bedroom was dry and the bed in Matthew's room had only one damp corner. It was pitch dark and still raining and nothing could be done. I knew that I would need all my energy the following day and so, after covering our bed with plastic sheets, just in case, we tried to sleep.

The following morning as I opened my eyes to already strong sunlight I wondered briefly what I was doing in the other bedroom. We soon discovered what had happened. The top half of our chimney had been blown off and had crashed through the roof. There were broken tiles everywhere. We dragged all our sodden furniture out into the blessed sun and mopped the floors, pushing the water out of the house on each side. It was exhausting and, I found, curiously depressing, as though one had been singled out for punishment by the gods, a totally irrational but very powerful feeling.

All morning we worked. Sooty water had streaked the wall soaking clothes, books and foodstuff. Suddenly we realised that we had seen nothing of Raymond or Claudette. They invariably appeared to share with us anything unusual. While Mike drove down to the farm I went into the garden and saw that several of the great branches on the west side of the ash tree had been torn off. I then realised that they were lying scattered some hundred yards away up the field toward the wood. Coming round to the south-facing garden I saw the shredded leaves on my sumach trees, even the Virginia creeper was full of holes.

Mike returned to describe the devastation on the farm. He had found Claudette weeping in the courtyard, Raymond trying to comfort her and, twelve hours after the storm, there was still a high drift of hailstones against the wall of the farmhouse. The tornado had cut a swathe across the land as it advanced from the south.

'The noise!' Claudette shuddered. 'It only lasted a few minutes but I'll never forget the noise.' We surveyed the damage and then I understood why they had always talked about hail, *la grêle*, with such fear. In the largest plum orchard where hardly one tree was undamaged, branches and fruit littered the ground. Any fruit still on the trees was cut to pieces and the maize in the next field shredded. The tall, forty-year-old pine trees, planted to protect the orchard, had been twisted out and hurled down. Roof tiles were everywhere, barns blown down and fences blown completely away. Our hole in the roof seemed trivial by comparison.

For days afterwards all one could hear were sounds of hammers and saws. Adam and Mike mended our roof, replacing all the broken tiles. The chimney had to wait until the winter as M. René was working every daylight hour. Although this was our first such experience, sudden local hailstorms are not unknown in the region. Grandpa told us that when he was a boy the church bells would be rung and farmers living on high ground would try to fire rockets into the storm clouds to prevent them spiralling upwards and then, as they cooled, falling as hail. More recently, they had experimented with hiring light aircraft to attempt to disperse the clouds but, as this was expensive and not particularly successful they finally gave up the struggle to control the elements and settled for insurance. 'But they only pay me for one harvest,' said Raymond. 'It's taken me fifteen years to get that orchard so beautiful. Now look at it. No amount of money can compensate for that.'

'I'm sorry to have to bid you farewell without the light in my eyes,' he said to Adam the following day, as he and Cas left for England. The violence of the storm had sorely tested his normal stoicism and had stunned us all.

Whenever the weather kept us indoors we got out the hat box. As we gradually sorted out those letters which were in one piece a cast of characters assembled to intrigue us, Alphonse and Delphine, Henri Mauriac, Fernand, Clothilde, who were they all? Matthew was interested in a small, faded photograph of a soldier in a red velvet frame, the number 20 clearly visible on his collar. He stands proudly, his epauletted shoulders squared, a cigarette deliberately poised between thumb and forefinger. He thought this might be Justin and was proved right when, at the bottom of the box, we found a certificate of good conduct from the 20th Infantry Regiment which, the date of birth being November 26, 1866, had clearly belonged to Justin, although it seemed that he had been chistened Jean. Here was his description; 1.67 metres tall with brown hair and eyes, an oval face, a long nose and a pointed chin.

We found a touching letter from a child to her Grandfather, presumably old Sieur Pierre Costes, written in 1911 and signed Esther. 'Of course she's Esther Blanc now,' said Grandma casually.

'She's still alive?' This was unexpected good luck.

'Very much so. She's eighty-three now but she partners Grandpa at whist every other Thursday. You should talk to her. I'll arrange it.' A few days later Grandma and I were eating sponge cakes and drinking sweet white wine with Esther Blanc in her little house in the next village where she has lived since she was born. Her mind was sharp but like many old people, she leaped from the past to the present and back again without warning and she spoke so fast that I found her difficult to follow.

She did confirm that the photograph was Justin. 'There were three brothers,' she said. 'My father, Célestin, was the youngest. They were all born at Bel-Air and their mother died in childbirth, it would have been a girl.' She looked with affection at the picture of Anaïs and her son, which I had brought with me. 'Ah what a good woman she was,' she said. 'I remember her much better than my Uncle Justin of course, she was *vaillante*.' She explained that she had been far too burdened with looking after her own aged parents and those of her husband to care for her Aunt and cousin when they grew old. Then I realised that this, of course, was *la nièce* of whom Raymond had spoken when he had told me about the life annuity agreement with which he had acquired Bel-Air.

This summer Mme Esther came up to visit our house which she had not seen since Anaïs's funeral in 1963. As she stepped through the door she smiled delightedly round her. '*Ah, vous avez gardé le buffet de ma Tante et sa table,*' she murmured, rubbing her frail hand across the surface, given an extra polish for the occasion. 'This house was always spotless,' she said firmly. '*Ma tante* was most particular.' She looked approvingly at the photograph now hung on the wall. I offered her white wine or tea with lemon. Surprisingly she accepted the tea and ate a rock-cake with obvious pleasure. She found it good and as she ate she remembered a story her father had told her about himself and his two brothers being woken in the night at Bel-Air by the glow of a huge fire, a barn burning not too far away. Terrified, they called their father but he was not at home. It was then that they discovered from their nearest neighbours their father's habit of waiting until his boys were asleep before setting off across the fields to visit his mistress at a distant farm. Mme Esther chuckled. 'That was the night they got found out.'

She sat reminiscing for over an hour while I cursed my inadequate French and wished she would speak more slowly. She did try but after the first sentence she would forget and the words would tumble out at ever increasing speed. I had found a letter in its black-edged envelope which she had written to Anaïs in 1919, the year of Justin's death. *Je n'ose vous dire ces mots qui sembleraient cruellement ironiques et vides de sens: Bonne année*, she had written. Mme Esther re-read her own words after so many years and wiped her eyes. 'Ah madame,' she said, 'there are many sadnesses in life, are there not? I too lost my husband with cancer and also my daughter. My son too has been ill but, thank God, he is getting better,' she smiled.

A car turned into our drive and a child's footsteps ran up to the porch. It was Mme Esther's daughter-in-law and grand child come to fetch her. The old lady hauled herself stiffly out of the chair to embrace the small brown-limbed girl who stood gazing round the room sucking her finger. In her striped tee-shirt and luminous trainers she blew away the shadows of the past and jolted us back to the present. 'This is my Natalie,' said her grandmother proudly. 'I have four grandchildren, they keep me young.' Together we walked to the car and before leaving she turned to look at Bel-Air. '*Ma tante* Anaïs, she loved this house,' she said firmly, anxiously almost. 'I know,' I replied, 'I've always known.'

13

*T*he next summer, having been spoilt by the flight to Toulouse but needing a car in France, we sought ways of making the journey less arduous. At six o'clock one evening we put the car on the train at Boulogne, ate a picnic, slept peacefully all night and awoke refreshed to breakfast in the station buffet at Brive, in the Dordogne, at five o' clock. All that remained was a few hours of leisurely driving through glorious countryside in the early dawn.

We had always previously avoided the town of Rocamadour, knowing it to be like any shrine in the tourist season, crammed with visitors and charabancs. Now we took a chance and, slipping in quietly before seven, found it deserted. Alone we climbed the great stone staircase where thousands of pilgrims have passed, some on their knees to expiate a crime, and found at the top, by great good luck, a friendly woman who was just about to clean the chapel of the Dark Virgin. We stood, the three of us and the vacuum cleaner, for a few moments of silence before the simple wooden statue with her compelling smile.

This was the first summer that we really began to notice the northward march of the sunflowers. Previously confined to Van Gogh country they had already begun to move west to the valley of the Garonne. Now we saw their huge green heads in bud in the Dordogne, oddly out of place in this region of sombre valleys and castled crags. As we drew nearer to our village we saw that some of our neighbouring farmers had also planted *les tournesols*. We wondered about Bel-Air. Normally we would have known what Raymond had planted that spring but, determined that the danger of having a second home and never going anywhere else must be avoided, we had taken our early holiday in Crete.

As we drove into our village we stopped to greet Mme Barrou who was weeding yet another crop of carrots. Proferring the back of her muddy hand through the car window she beamed, '*Eh alors, vous êtes arrivés . . . très bien.*' We discussed the weather and the crops. No, she hadn't planted sunflowers, she was waiting to see how the others got on. We started to go. '*Attendez, attendez,*' she yelled, and two large bunches of carrots fell onto the back seat of the car.

Raymond had one field of sunflowers to see how they yielded but it was ripe wheat which covered *le grand champ* in a sea of shimmering bronze. At the side of our track, waiting for the combine harvester to arrive, lay the long green container for the grain. 'When will she come, *la moissoneuse*?' we asked.

'*Demain ou après-demain s'il ne pleut pas pendant la nuit,*' Raymond answered, looking anxiously at the sky. I could see no sign of rain. The night was hot. The thermometer on our porch read 79 degrees when we went to bed, but by the next morning pale clouds drifted across and there was the sound of distant thunder. The smell of grain was sweet on the stormy air for *la moissoneuse* had started early and we knew that as long as the rain held off she would trundle back and forth until the field was finished. Happily all the corn was harvested before three nights of heavy rain were each followed by brilliantly sunny days. The earth steamed, growth was so rapid as to be almost visible, and the distant fields of sunflowers changed from a golden flecked green to a blaze of yellow.

A strange bird flew into the house. Panic stricken it beat its wings in a frenzy to escape and we opened every door and window trying to assist it. Later as we described it to Raymond he said that it sounded like a quail. 'If it was *la caille*,' he grinned, 'it would have been better to have opened the door of the oven.' The next day we heard the quail's strange 'whoop whoop whoop' call across the fields and he told us the old saying that the more times she repeated her call, the higher would be the yield of corn.

The old, clacking baler had been put away in one of Raymond's many barns to become another machine *d'autrefois*. After the combine harvester another new monster munched *le grand champ* in a tenth of the time, turning the straw into giant rounds, seven feet high, which waited solemnly to be collected. Raymond bought a great two-pronged *fourche*, which transformed the tractor into a dangerous stag beetle. He came up to Bel-Air to show it to Mike, clearly hoping for some moral, if not physical, support while he tried it out. Mike, always happy to drive a tractor and trailer, disappeared and I watched them working together, Raymond, with lowered *fourche*, charging the bales and once they were impaled, levering them up onto the trailer.

When the straw had been in small bales we had all helped to stack them neatly in the barn. We tossed them from the trailer onto a *monte-charge*, a mounting conveyor belt, which, as the stack grew higher, carried them to the top of the barn where Raymond arranged them in neat row after row. Inside the barn the temperature rose as the sun-drenched straw filled every space. He took great pride in having his barns in impeccable order. Now it was quicker but much more difficult. When, after an hour of manoeuvering the massive rounds with *la fourche*, Raymond surveyed the tall, off-centre columns, his face was glum. '*Ce n'est pas aussi joli que d'habitude*,' he said sadly, as he shut the barn doors. Other things were changing too. He grew no tobacco that year. It was partly the low prices the dealers were paying but also a matter of conscience. Grandpa was becoming frailer and worked less in the fields. He spent a great deal of time checking the fences and making sure that the cows had water.

We decided to convert our old prune oven on the west side of the house into a small studio. The hedgehogs had found another home and we stacked the wood in Raymond's barn. Mike had taken early retirement and was increasingly busy writing and illustrating children's books. Since all our visitors congregated just outside the front porch for breakfast and then moved gradually eastwards, we thought it might make a quiet haven. M. René, also now officially retired but happy as ever to earn *argent liquide*, came one morning for consultations bringing with him le Barbu, his new assistant. A Spanish Basque with a silvery beard a foot long, he had lived locally for over twenty years but his French was so idiosyncratic that it took a great deal of getting used to. Although in his early sixties, le Barbu was lithe and energetic. He drank no alcohol and would work, apart from the usual two hour break at midday, from eight in the morning to eight at night with no sign of fatigue.

M. René was in the process of helping him to build a house which was almost finished. Le Barbu, having run out of funds, now worked for M. René who paid him, not in cash but in materials and labour. 'Where is your house?' we enquired.

'Oh, not far from the Château,' he said. 'There was *une très vieille maison* there on the lane but it was a ruin – falling down. I've used a lot of the stones and of course I have to keep the old name. It's called *La Cavalière*. This was an odd coincidence for on one of Adam's early visits to Bel-Air he had roamed the countryside with a camera and the place which had most fascinated him, and to which he had later taken me, was this same ruin near the Château. I remembered the pear tree which grew through the roof. At supper one evening he described its haunted atmosphere to Raymond, telling him of a crumbling, ex-army greatcoat which still hung behind the door. 'the last person to live there,' said Raymond, 'was a Polish refugee from the war. The house is called *La Cavalière.*' But that was not all. We had recently managed to decipher the oldest documents in the hat-box, finding that they pre-dated the Revolution and they concerned one Pierre St Antoine Laroque. In various contracts written in 1758, 1765 and 1768 he is reminded that he must pay *les impositions Royales* and *la rente au Seigneur*. The next document, written in the seventh year of the Republic and dated *le dix-neuf Prarial*, the new name for June in the Revolutionary calendar, concerns his son, *Citoyen Jean Roquer demeurant au lieu appelé La Cavalière*. Now, working with us at Bel-Air was le Barbu who had finally demolished everything except the name, *La Cavalière*.

The work on our new *atelier* began with deliveries of sand and gravel which M. René typically dumped in the least convenient place, right in the path of anyone wishing to unroll the hose to water the garden. There were two small openings in the walls of the prune oven, one where the chimney had protruded, which we filled, the other, a small window about ten inches square, covered in Virginia creeper, which we planned to enlarge. As we hacked down the creeper and dug out the roots, as thick as arms and with laterals ten feet long, we discovered that they had penetrated into the drain which took away the clean water. When we pulled out the solid, woven mesh we understood why the creeper flourished so abundantly and the bath water took so long to run away.

We bought a simple, ready-made wooden windowframe and chose a section of an old oak beam for a lintel. We imagined that M. René would first knock out just enough of the wall to insert the lintel before enlarging the hole for the window, but nothing so simple. Le Barbu who, I then learned with some unease, was by trade a shepherd, pounded away with a crow bar until it seemed to me that there was a hole large enough for two windows. The pile of stones from the wall grew higher. Just as I felt that the whole structure might well collapse, they decided that it might be the moment to put in the heavy lintel, and with many a groan and cry they inched it up. Then the wiry little shepherd appeared to be supporting most of the weight on his back while M. René struggled with two well-worn adjustable props which he had clearly forgotten to check before this precise moment. *'Ah malheur!'* he repeated, the sweat rolling down his fat red face. The corroded pegs were reluctant to budge. Le Barbu said nothing.

Each day they made an early start as by four in the afternoon the sun had moved round to beat on their backs. We noticed that M. René had begun to set the window in with grey cement and were glad that we were there. He cheerfully admitted that a cream colour would be more attractive and, unperturbed, drove off some eight miles to get it while we rigged up a tarpaulin to protect both them and the cement from the blazing heat. The window finished and the rebuilt wall cemented we were pleased with the result. The other interior wall we decided to leave *pierres apparentes* like the one in our bedroom and we asked M. René about having them both sandblasted.

A few days later the machine and its operator arrived. Protected by thick gloves and a sort of diver's helmet, inch by inch he began to clean the wall of the new *atelier* and also the high narrow pine doors which began to look very handsome. The following day he planned to do the wall in our bedroom. We had cleared the room by the time M. René arrived, bringing a large roll of plastic which he cut into lengths. He and Mike stapled them over the window and doors but unfortunately they missed a long, hairline crack between the door frame and the wall into the living-room. I was sitting at the table when the sandblasting began and after the first twenty minutes had become accustomed to the noise in the next room. The operator suddenly changed direction and down the whole length of the unsuspected crack a jet of sand blasted into the living room, covering everything, including me. In seconds the air was full of it, the room like a scene from Lawrence of Arabia, but my yells were inaudible and it was not until I had run right round the house to the door of the bedroom that they stopped the machine. And the next day we were expecting guests! That night, by the time we had washed all the china on the dresser – each cup contained a tablespoon of sand – shaken out every book, cleaned the cooker and every surface and swept about three feet of surprisingly heavy sand from our bedroom floor we were exhausted; but the wall looked good.

For the next two days M. René and le Barbu patiently pointed the stones with a cream cement leaving them proud, as asked, and we were pleased with the whole project. The new *atelier* had a splendid view. It now needed a floor and we planned to tile it with a terracotta brick which we would extend to cover the whole porch area – but that could wait until the following spring. We had to admit that we no longer had the same energy as when we first bought Bel-Air.

We lazed in the sun and swam in our friends' pool. More new friends, this time an English couple, Ruth and Edward Thomas, had a house about two miles away. Extremely rich and even more generous, their hospitality was lavish and unbounded and they invited us and any of our friends to use their beautiful pool. We introduced Raymond and Claudette and this year Raymond has finally conquered a very real fear of water and begun to swim. After his first few strokes he laughed aloud for sheer delight. '*C'est incroyable! Quelle sensation, c'est bizarre,*' he said, shaking the water from his ears. '*Eh Claudette, regarde, regarde,*' he cried, plunging in once more.

In Monflanquin posters went up for a performance of Molière's *L'Avare*, The Miser, which was to be held in the square at the summit of the town, using the church wall as a back drop. The company *Les Baladins D'Agenais* tour the whole south-west region during the summer and our town was to get one performance. Had *les Bertrand* seen them before? Were they any good? Raymond shrugged. He had no idea, but if we were going they would like to come.

Billed to start at nine o'clock, half an hour later a small

army of technicians was still making sound and lighting checks. The audience of about a hundred and fifty, many seated on wooden benches, were getting restless and I wondered what we had let ourselves in for. Suddenly it was dark, the lights came up, music began and streaming out from the house of the Black Prince came a wonderfully costumed troupe of actors. Running, leaping, cartwheeling, walking on their hands, they were so skilled in the style of the Commedia del Arte that they took our breath away. The set was a high wooden scaffolding with a staircase on each side and downstage a simple wooden step ladder, the steps facing the audience.

Much of the first scene which takes place between the daughter and her lover was played while swinging high on the scaffolding, without for one moment impairing the speaking. The girl often hung upside down and just as it seemed that her delicious breasts must tumble out of her low cut dress she would swing upright again as the audience sighed. Crouched motionless at the top of the tall stepladder, his back to the audience, sat the miser. When he first turned to reveal the grotesque white face, black lines on either side of the mouth, the crowd gasped. With infinite slowness, back braced against the steps, he began to descend the ladder like a malevolent spider, extending his thin black legs and flexing his bony fingers. In the scene where he discovers that his money has been stolen he scuttled into the audience, an anguished and desperate figure. The children shrieked and cried 'Non! Non!' when he demanded if one of them had stolen his treasure, but no one laughed. It was a masterly performance and the crowd applauded and cheered.

'C'était quelque chose,' said Grandma as we walked down to the car. Since then we have tried not to miss any of their performances, which included a pageant on the life of Eleanor of Aquitaine played in the now dry moat of the great Château of Bonaquil. The setting was spectacular, they used the battlements and towers, and the great horses which they rode in and out added most powerfully to both sound and smell.

As August ended another scent was beginning to fill the air. Ripening plums were once again weighing down the branches and this year we would inaugurate another new machine. Raymond had talked about it the previous year. Designed and manufactured locally, *la nouvelle machine pour les prunes* apparently shook and collected the fruit at speed. 'It's a marvellous invention, marvellous,' Raymond had declared. 'It will do the work in half the time.' Grandpa had said nothing, just pursed his mouth and wrinkled up his thin nose as though there was a bad smell somewhere.

We cleared the ground of the few plums that had fallen in the night and awaited the arrival of *la machine*. A triumphant, yet clearly nervous, Raymond appeared, his tongue wagging wildly as he tried to manoeuvre into position what looked like a giant grasshopper with red legs and folded green wings trailing behind the tractor. He backed it eventually to touch the first tree in the row and at the pull of a lever a claw grasped the slender trunk. '*Attention!*' he yelled as suddenly the great wings unfurled to encircle the tree with an upside down umbrella five metres across. At the touch of a third lever the tree shook and shuddered as if in ecstasy, the leaves in a frenzy as the lavender-coloured plums pelted into the green canopy and then tumbled through the central holes into the bright red containers beneath. Once empty the umbrella swiftly refolded and *la machine* moved to the next tree while we, the humble retinue, bent to retrieve the few plums that had fallen off the edge. It was a pretty spectacular performance.

All went well and Raymond was beginning to relax a little until we came to the end of the row. A small branch, hanging very low with fruit, obstructed the unfurling. Before it could be lifted clear it was ripped off by the force of the umbrella. Throwing his arms in the air and cursing loudly Raymond jumped from the tractor, picking up the torn branch as tenderly as though it were a human limb. '*Ah, il y a des défauts,'* he said sadly, looking at his new toy.

Claudette comforted him, *'Oh il y a toujours des défauts.'*

'C'est vrai. C'est vrai.' Reassured he climbed back and began again.

It was certainly all much quicker. There were far fewer of us and yet by midday we had harvested almost two tonnes of plums and were finished. The small plastic crates into which we had emptied our baskets in previous years had been replaced by great wooden *paloxes* each holding two hundred kilos which had to be loaded with the fork lift – another tricky manoeuvre – instead of being nonchalantly swung onto the trailer by M. Demoli's strong brown arms. M. Demoli was, sadly, absent. We had hardly glimpsed him all summer. His wife, not unreasonably, had grown weary of living in a hovel and had accepted the offer of a neat, new, council bungalow on the edge of Monflanquin. He had refused to go. Even worse, the scrap dealer for whom he had worked on an extremely freelance basis, in the winter, had suddenly moved to another district. Unable to cope with two desertions, M. Demoli, it was said, had taken to his bed and no one could get him out of it. Raymond, with typical kindness, had tried but even he had given up. Fernande, his wife, unperturbable as ever, worked with us and admired the new machine but the days of pelting her with plums were now *quelles d'autrefois*.

After lunch a delighted Raymond drove out of the courtyard to take his loaded trailer to the *Coopérative* where the plums would be dried. Before getting the machine he would have worked all afternoon climbing up and down the iron ladder to shake by hand and was often so tired at night that he would fall asleep over his supper. The weather was glorious and all the talk of the bumper harvest. Neighbours came to admire *la nouvelle machine* and everyone, except Grandpa, was delighted.

However, several days later Raymond returned from the *Coopérative* in a state of shock. There were too many plums! He was not the only farmer to have planted more trees in the last seven years, trees that were fruiting fully for the first time, nor was he the only one to have bought a machine. The *Coopérative*, though working flat out both night and day, simply did not have enough ovens to dry all the plums and they had decided to limit each *producteur* to two crates a day. It seemed there might be a plum mountain. What could be done? Each day some ripe plums would fall whether the trees were shaken or not, but that night there was a strong wind which blew in from the west and by next morning a gentle but persistent rain was drenching a thick carpet of plums. They would rot if they were left but the machine could not be used.

With raised voices and anguished gestures telephone calls were made. Distant cousins arrived to help and very old, rarely seen neighbours put on galoshes and ancient oilskins and crept out to join them. While *la machine* stood idly by with folded wings we picked up the plums in the way they had always been picked. Grandma had often talked about the problems of harvesting plums in the rain. This was our first such experience and, as we scraped the mud off our leaden boots for the tenth time we knew what she meant. The rain, now heavy enough to penetrate the trees, dripped relentlessly down our bent necks.

Once the two crates were full Raymond drove them glumly away while Claudette unearthed a few dozen of the smaller plastic crates which, by midday, we had filled. We loaded them and took them down to the farm.

The ancient *étuve* was already alight, smoke rising, a triumphant Grandpa replenishing the wood. As soon as he had heard the news he had lit it, knowing that the drying of the remainder of the plums would be up to him. Grandma laid out the flat wooden trays on two long planks supported on oil drums and we tipped the wet sticky plums in, pressing them down gently into the corners. Once they were filled Mike helped Grandpa to load the *wagonet* and push it into the heat. As the first load began to dry Grandma was already filling the next lot of trays. Their *système* needed once more, they were content. From every farm spirals of smoke arose from *étuves* that had long been abandoned but were now reborn.

At last the backlog was cleared. The *Coopérative* once more accepted as many crates as the farmers could deliver and there was talk of adding another oven before next year. The crisis was over. The weather returned to normal and the new machine once more unfurled its great green umbrella beneath the trees. The little iron ladder was reserved for those too fragile for its rough embrace. Mike stayed to help whenever Raymond needed a driver for the fork lift but I went back to work in my garden. For me the charm of harvesting plums had been the peace of the orchards, the quiet chatter under the trees and the sweet smell of warm fruit.

La machine necessitated much yelling of 'STOP' as it was positioned and the fumes from the old tractor which pulled it lingered under the low trees. Yet another harvest had become *quelque chose d'autrefois*. Raymond felt it. Proud though he was of his machine he regretted the passing of another tradition.

'But what else can I do?' he said. 'My parents-in-law are old and my children?' he shrugged. Philippe was studying economics at college in Bordeaux and Véronique was learning office skills. Neither was interested in a career as a farmer. *'Eh alors,'* he said, *'il faut acheter les machines.'*

But in the warm, wet woods, under the ageless layers of leaf mould another harvest waited that needed no machines. Two spells of heavy rain followed by long, hot days had begun a relentless underground movement, soon to reveal itself. Grandpa had already taken to disappearing between the trees in the early morning mist. When we commented he smiled, tapped the side of his nose, raised his eyebrows and said 'In a few days.'

It was the beginning of the season of the *Boletus edulis* or *le cèpe de Bordeaux* and its imminent arrival was the signal for a frenzy of searching in the steaming woods. On our early morning trips to market there were cars parked along the edges of the wooded lanes and signs *CHAMPIGNONS*

INTERDIT began to appear nailed to the trees. '*C'est la guerre,*' said Raymond. 'If you get up at seven your neighbour will get up at six.' It sounded to me very much like the three little pigs.

One morning, well before eight, Claudette in her flowered hat, apron and wellingtons and carrying a long stick, arrived on our porch. Flushed with excitement she opened her carrier bag to show us a dozen or so brownish-orange tops with thick white stalks which broadened at the base. Some six inches across, others no bigger than her thumb, she took each one out as tenderly as though it were alive, laying them on the well cover before sitting down to drink coffee. She admitted that it was the fascination of finding, even more than the eating of these white fleshed edible toadstools that obsessed her. '*C'est la passion,*' she laughed.

Normally too busy to take even an afternoon off, once the *cèpes* had begun she neglected the farm and spent hours in the woods. '*Elle est toujours comme ça,*' said Raymond in apparent indulgence, except that *his* passion is eating them. We were invited to try them, a whole dish full, freshly picked and cooked crisp. '*Sentez, sentez,*' said Raymond, in a kind of ecstasy. 'When they are cooking they perfume the whole house.' I really felt quite guilty. They were perfectly edible but, try as I might, their appeal was lost on me. '*Oh, c'est une question d'habitude,*' he said kindly.

The excitement of finding them was something I could understand. Into a soft, humid world of dappled light and shadows, the very concentration of looking, adjusting one's eyes to each patch of patterned ground, turning the leaves gently with a stick and circling round and round, anxious not to miss an inch, was mesmeric.

The wood was full of fungi, underfoot and hanging like thick, leathery lips from the trunks of the trees, but, by now, we knew what we were looking for. Each worked in their own small section but at the first cry we would converge for the *cèpes* were always in a cluster, some clearly visible above ground, others just the faintest concavity beneath the thick carpet of leaves. We pulled them gently and then tried to remember the exact location, for tomorrow there would be more – if we managed to get there first.

With no arduous preparation of the ground, no expensive fertilisers or seed, no watering or weeding, I could understand the fascination of such a harvest for the farmer. It was a gift from the gods and that year was especially bountiful. Grandpa returned one morning with several kilos and refused to tell anyone where he had found them.

The biggest joke in the neighbourhood was old M. Boulloner, a retired Parisien, not the most popular person in our village. Each day he would bump slowly up the track to the woods in his red car. On one occasion he couldn't find the way out of the wood and had to be rescued. Each evening he would return with a bulging carrier bag which, wisely, he would take down to the farm for Raymond to check. With cries of '*Mauvais, mauvais,*' Raymond would reject one after the other until poor M. Boulloner was lucky to be left with one miserable mushroom for his evening omelette. Sadly, his smart city cap on his head and his sleek little dachshund at his heels, he would plod out to the car.

'Poor M. Boulloner,' I said.

'*Huh, les Parisiens,*' Raymond was unusually unsympathetic. 'What do they know about *la campagne*? I remember when I was trying to sell Bel-Air the agent said to me, "You'd do far better to sell it to *les Anglais que les Parisiens*." ' He suddenly smiled at me, surprised, 'She was right, wasn't she?'

14

CARTE-LETTRE
DE L'ESPÉRANCE

Mr Castes Justin

Un brave Poilu

*D*id you ever know someone called Alphonse?' I asked
Grandma as we sat together one day shelling *coco* beans for
bottling.

She lifted her head and smiled at me. 'Those old letters
again, I suppose?' she said. Deciphering the letters in the
hat box was still a never-ending fascination, and so many
of them were written during the Great War.

'Alphonse?' Grandma's busy hands stilled and her small
face wrinkled up like an end-of-season apple. 'I never knew
Alphonse but I think he was married to Delphine.'

'That's right,' I said, 'and who was Delphine?'

'Delphine was a friend of Anaïs.' I waited. 'She used to
write to her.' I nodded encouragingly. Grandma must not
be hurried. 'They'd gone away long before I came here to
be married but I've often heard Anaïs talk about her. She
was in service at *Au Bosc*.'

'It looks as though Anaïs sent Alphonse food parcels
when he was in the army in the first war,' I said.

'*C'est possible*,' said Grandma, and got on with the beans.

165

'*Grande était ma surprise hier soir,*' begins Alphonse expansively, in a letter from Secteur Postal 145, dated August 20 1916, 'to find your unexpected parcel. The *civet* was excellent.' I imagined Anaïs filling a bottling jar with perhaps *civet de lièvre*, which Grandma sometimes makes when one of the few remaining hares is inevitably flushed out by a *chausseur*.

But the letter continues, 'My comrades with whom I shared it wish to send their felicitations to the cook.' Clearly it was a large *civet*. How on earth did she pack it? In his other letter Alphonse thanks Anaïs and Justin for *un bon morceau* which will be eaten '*en Champagne dans le pays où les canons sont en action et les permissions suprimées,*' leave cancelled. As I became familiar with the names of these reluctant soldiers I wished that the mice had not ravaged so many of their letters. Some used for ancient nests fell into shreds as we lifted them from the box. Fortunately many were still intact and with dictionary and magnifying glass I began to learn a little about what life was like during the Great War.

There were several letters from Anaïs's brother, one Henri Mauriac who was with the 130th Territorial Brigade. He begins cheerfully enough on a postcard marked *Correspondance des Armées Françaises*. It has a design of an optimistic looking soldier, hands clasped on his upturned rifle, as he stands against a background of crossed tricolours. Henri hopes to see his sister, brother-in-law and nephew Alaïs before too long and sends them all *une bonne poignée de main*, a good handshake, but as the war continues his letters change. In civilian life he may have been a chef, for in January 1916 he writes that at least cooking, *mon ancien métier*, is helping to make the winter, with its constant skirmishes, endurable. He hopes that it will all end soon, '*c'est mauvais la guerre.*'

Anaïs is also sending him parcels and his letter of May 29, 1916 thanks her for her present. Financially he is doing rather well, he says, as he has almost no expenses and nothing on which to spend his pay. Under canvas in a wood he is safe from shelling but he writes, 'by the time this letter arrives *je serai pour sûr a la côte du poivre*, a name that you will have already seen in the papers.' I assume that this must be a euphemism for the hottest part of the front line, something like Hell-fire Corner.

By July Uncle Henri Mauriac is back near Soissons where, in spite of sporadic gunfire, he wishes he could stay for the duration. He is still in a bad state as a result of his recent experiences *'ce que j'ai vu autrefois,'* and in his letter of October he writes 'Nothing changes, this life has disgusted me now for a long time and there is no sign of an end to it.' Imminent leave temporarily cheers him in November when he hopes to *'mettre pied à terre chez vous'* on the evening of the 13th. But sadly he does not manage to see his sister as he has unexpectedly to travel home via Bordeaux. He writes later to tell her that he tried to see them on market day at Monflanquin, which ever since 1256 has been held on a Thursday morning. But he arrived very late and they, presumably not knowing that he might come, had already left. He explains how the few days of leave flew by, especially since he had to plant his seeds, nothing having been done while he was away. He finishes by saying that he is back at Soissons but not for long. 'If this goes on much longer I can assure you one would be better off dead,' he adds bitterly.

The preoccupation with work needing to be done on the land is clear in another letter written in 1916 by a neighbour, M. Coupé, a gendarme attached to the British Army. *'Cher et brave Anaïs,'* he writes, 'as soon as possible would you please prune my plum trees, taking care not to strip them too bare.' He writes of the dreadful wet weather and of the *'Canadiens, Australiens, Ecossais et les Anglais chantant constamment jouant leur belle musique'*. This puzzled me until an expert on the First World War explained to me that the French considered the habit of the British army to march everywhere to music extremely odd. They had regimental bands but they were not sent to the front line.

M. Coupé continues, 'At the moment I have a droll task.

Each morning before daybreak, myself and another gendarme enter an unhappy village, so bombarded as to be almost demolished. We hide in the cellars and at dusk we return to the billet where we must report the exact number of fallen shells. Needless to say we are excused inspection,' he adds wryly. My expert again explained that these would have been enemy shells which were counted because each new gun crew taking over an emplacement fired off twice as many shells to check their range. In this way enemy troop change-overs could be checked.

By far the largest group of wartime letters was written in an almost illegible hand. The letters spanned two years and were from one Fernand Lacoste. He was Anaïs's nephew and something of a hero and confidant to Alaïs, his handicapped cousin. He mentions his wife, Clothilde, who lives at Viallette. This was interesting to us as Viallette is about a kilometre from Bel-Air. When the trees are bare we can see the roof. In 1976 when we first came, it was a shell without floors. Only the roof had been repaired to stop the walls from crumbling away. Now it is being lovingly restored by, unusually, a French couple who, tiring of town life, have made it their home. He is a lecturer in a technical college and he works on this long-term project in the vacation. They raise a few sheep and chicken as a side line.

Fernand Lacoste, the earlier inhabitant of Viallette, wrote many letters in his small, cramped hand. I assume that paper and ink was expensive but, in those days of oil-lamps and candles, I wonder how difficult they were to read. There are twenty-five letters, written between January 1916 and August 1918, which give interesting glimpses of the war and also of his relationship with his, I assume, younger, and certainly less worldly cousin, Alaïs, at Bel-Air.

In January he writes that he has changed his billet and that although very draughty it is better than the trenches. He finishes affectionately '*Reçoit douceur et bons baisers de ton cousin.*' By September, realising that the war will not be quickly won, he forsees at least another winter of fighting. Anaïs has been sending more food parcels. As I read, I imagined the whole of France criss-crossed with *civets* and *saucissons*. Fernand thanks his Aunt for *le bon morceau* which he has tasted but is saving for Sunday, when he will have a feast before leaving for eight days at the front, having already endured four days of shelling. 'I am up to my stomach in mud,' he writes, ending wistfully, 'the grapes at home must be ripening'.

The next letter which survives was written in the following January and seems to be in answer to a letter from Alaïs about some romantic problem. Fernand describes *'les jeunes filles'* as having to make themselves agreeable *'à ceux qui restent et n'ont pas trop besoin de le faire difficile'*. He warns Alaïs against talking about any conquest that he might make, but also tells him that it is high time that he found himself a girl. He speaks bitterly of having to abandon his own love to go to war and concludes by promising to bring his cousin a lighter when he next has leave.

Whatever amorous pursuits Alaïs was engaged in were cut short by his own sudden and unexpected call-up sometime in May 1917. He was sent to the barracks at Montauban where he was very unhappy and constantly trying to convince the Army that he was sufficiently handicapped to be invalided out. The first mention of his conscription is in a letter that he received from Fernand's wife Clothilde, at Viallette. She tells him that his mother walked down through the fields from Bel-Air bringing her son's letters, and explaining that his call-up must be a mistake. Clothilde writes, 'you will not have to stay long. I wish you luck and a speedy return. I shall write to tell Fernand what has happened.' She ends by thanking Alaïs for his *'jolie carte. Tu as un jolis logement.'* I doubt if poor Alaïs considered his barracks in this way.

His cousin Fernand writes, appropriately on *une carte lettre de l'espérance*, and tries both to cheer and to warn him. 'I got your card,' he writes, 'and I can see that you don't find *ce metier trop désagréable*. Do your best to keep your bosses happy for it's what you do to begin with which will make all the difference to the way you are treated.' Two days later

Fernand writes to reassure his Aunt and Uncle that their son is not complaining too much, but from his letters to his mother it is clear that it was only to cousin Fernand that Alaïs kept up a brave face. He was only at Montauban for about a month but in that time there are sixteen letters written between mother and son.

His mother is also anxious for him not to complain to the authorities and get *une mauvaise note*, 'Tell me if you have enough bread,' she writes, 'and if you are *bien couchée*'. Once again she turns to her school book and has underlined the words that *La Petite Jeanne* uses to comfort her daughter when she must leave her. '*Quand j'ai perdu ton père, je ne suis pas morte, parce que j'ai pensé à vous, mes enfants; et tu penseras à moi pour te donner du courage.*'

Alaïs is angry at the questions he is asked by the board who assess his eligibility for invaliding out and his hopes of a discharge fade with every letter. He writes almost every day.

His mother reminds him, as no doubt others pointed out to her, that he is better off where he is than at the front, adding that they've had no news in the village of 'young Perault' for two weeks. Alaïs agrees but tells her just what he thinks about the noise, the awful soup, the mouldy bread as hard as wood, and the undercooked meat.

Uncle Henri Mauriac, clearly behind with the family news, writes to reassure his sister that poor Alaïs will not be called up. 'I've sent him your address to show him that you *did* have to go,' writes Anaïs crossly.'

On May 28 Alaïs has some contact with a sympathetic Brigadier who asks him details about the plum harvest. 'I told him I'd like to show him myself,' says Alaïs. On the last day of May he is at his most despondent. He is being made to march *commes les autres*. 'I would much rather be at home doing my one kilometre a day,' he writes. His mother tries to cheer him with snippets of local news. 'Your father is going to market to sell a horse. Delphine is selling a cow next week,' and sadly, 'Young Perault is dead. The news has just come.'

The letters of both mother and son are extremely difficult to understand as, apart from the minute writing, neither of them can spell. They most certainly would have talked patois together so that French was almost a second language. I have a copy of a beautifully written and faultlessly spelt letter from Anaïs to his mother, written when he was eleven years old and clearly copied from the blackboard, but fourteen years later and left to himself he writes as he speaks. *'C'est'* is *'sais'!*

At last the army decided that he was too handicapped to be much use and in his final triumphant letter of June 9 he writes, 'I still have a few more days left but on Monday or Wednesday I shall leave for Grèzelongue *et puis la guerre sera finie pour mois sais un salle metier*. It's a dirty business.'

'He never forgot the experience,' said Raymond, when I showed him some of the letters. 'I didn't realise that he was in for such a short time. He made it seem much longer when he talked about it.'

'Did you know Clothilde and Fernand?' I asked him.

'Clothilde?' he cried. *'Il faut demander à Mme Barrou,'* you must ask Mme Barrou – Clothilde was her aunt and lived with her until she died.

It was in the village shop that I next bumped into the champion carrot grower. *'Et alors,'* she shouted, embracing me fiercely. She had wide black rims of earth under her nails, and her hair, which looked as though she had trimmed it herself with the secateurs, showed a wide, white parting in the carrot coloured strands. *'Ça va?'*

'Ça va. I've been hoping to see you to talk about Clothilde. She was your aunt I hear.'

'Bien sûr. She was married to Fernand who was the son of Mathilde, who was the sister of Anaïs,' she finished triumphantly.

'And they lived at Viallette?' I asked. Mme Barrou nodded.

'What happened to Fernand?'

She said nothing but took me by the hand and led me across the road to the war memorial. I had seen it every time I came out of the shop and yet had never noticed his name. How Alaïs must have missed his hero and his confidant.

The last group of letters are from Delphine and although written later are full of references to the hideous war that changed so many lives. Most of her letters are very sad. The first one, written at the end of 1919, is the longest.

'I use the occasion of the new year to break our silence and offer to you my best wishes and also to Alaïs (by this time Justin was dead). I hope that 1920 will favour us both with health, prosperity and, above all, consolation. I think so often about you. There is no corner of your home that I cannot remember for I shall never forget that in those moments of loneliness and sadness that I went through during the war I came to you so many times to search for consolation.'

It seems that although she has moved, Delphine is still in service, and extremely unhappy. She tells Anaïs that she tries hard to remember her advice, in particular about keeping the linen in order, but that by the time she has finished her work it is gone nine o'clock and after having been on her feet all day she is too tired to sew. 'And I will not be a sou better off by the end of the year,' she writes, 'as everything gets dearer. I am obliged to believe that the best time of our life is past for we shall never be as contented as we were before the war. I shall stop my writing as I shall finish by boring you . . . She who never forgets you, Delphine.' Alphonse, who clearly did survive the war, adds a cheery postscript, wishing that Alaïs might find a charming other half.

Anaïs must have sent her many parcels over the years for almost every letter thanks her for some kindness. 'Thank you for the prunes. I eat them with so much more pleasure, knowing that they come from Grèzelongue.' 'Thank you for putting a flower in your letter, it brought me the perfume of Grèzelongue, and also for the money for the apron which will make me look more correct as you told me.' The last letter is written in January 1939, on the eve of yet another war, and ends 'I'm sorry not to have written for the new year but we had to kill the pig as he was lame. I shall never be young again and it is only bad days to come that await me. If I weren't so far away I could come and tell you my troubles as I did during the war.'

What happened to Delphine in the Second World War to end this correspondence of twenty years I shall probably never know.

Mme Barrou talked about Anaïs and her sister Mathilde going to church together, with Clothilde. 'They were always so neat and clean,' she said, 'and always with a sprig of something pinned to their coat, a little rose or a bit of heather.' One Sunday afternoon returning from a drive in Grandpa's old Citroen, Raymond took us to the churchyard where Anaïs, Justin and their son Alaïs are buried together. Now each summer I make a pilgrimage; I tidy the weeds and I plant a few more of Anaïs's house leeks, *sempervivum*. I hope eventually that they will cover the grave and make her last resting place ever green.

15

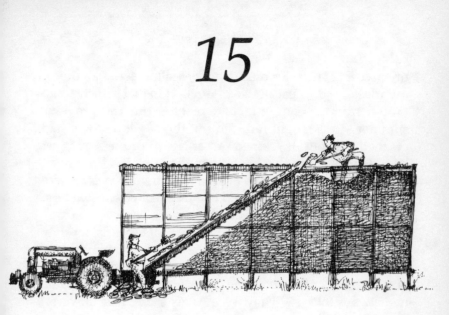

T his year we could not wait until July to return to Bel-Air. Our Cretan holiday of the previous year had been fun, with sunlight so bright in skies so vividly blue, that even before breaking our fast on thick yoghurt and honey, we had reached for sunglasses. The hillsides were an embroidery of flowers and the Cretans the most beautiful people with thick, lustrous hair which sprang from their foreheads as though they were perpetually emerging from the sea. But inevitably we, the tourists, were on the whole an unlovely lot, and I began to tire of enforced idleness and all those meek, red-kneed husbands with shopping bags, patiently trailing their bargain-seeking wives through endless curtains of cotton dresses, scarves and tablecloths.

We flew to Toulouse in May and the train to Agen was crammed with excited migrant workers coming to pick the strawberries. After an exceptionally mild and wet winter the grass round the house, full of scabious, poppies and clover, was up to my shoulders. In the south-facing lawn Raymond had kindly cut a rectangle but he had left a wide, untouched border for fear of inadvertently mowing down my invisible lavender bushes, my escallonia and japonica, my irises, and, most precious of all, a loquat which I had grown from a stone and had planted out the previous summer. The straight red stems of the passion flower had reached the roof. It seemed rather late to prune it so I just hoped that some of the flowers would tumble over and hang down. There were clumps of wild marguerites everywhere and in the dusk they gleamed like unattached, milky stars; but the biggest surprise was the roses.

We had never been at Bel-Air in late May. At Easter they had just begun to bud and by the time we came back in late July they were dry, tattered bushes which gave no hint of the beauty of the flowering. Now we saw what Grandma had always told us. 'They were Anaïs's favourite flowers,' she said. On the north-facing wall, the whole length of the *chai*, a brilliant cerise rose thrust its long, pointed buds up through the stems of the elderberry and orange blossom. A sweet-scented, double pale pink climber was held neatly in place on the west corner by the tall, sticky stems of common cleaver which, as children, we had called 'sweethearts' as we stuck them on each others' backs. Yet more, small red roses bloomed under the window of the new *atelier* and on the south-facing wall, what I had always thought was the remains of a dog-rose turned out to be a thick-petalled, creamy white, scented climber. And to think they had all been blooming for the last twelve years and we had never seen them.

And there were more birds. Hour after hour, hidden high in the ash tree, a warbler repeated his liquid, questioning trill. I kept the binoculars round my neck but I never saw him. In the wooden letter box which hangs next to the front door were seven eggs and the parents, a pair of great tits, fretted whenever we sat on the porch. Once the eggs were hatched we were obliged to move chairs and table from the flight path between the nest and the ash tree. Each time we came out of the door the thin, high piping would be instantly silenced by a fierce click from the parent but, once we were out of the way, juicy caterpillars were posted through the slit intended for the mail. We made a sign for the postman, '*Chez oiseaux. Posez les lettres sur la table SVP.*'

Outside the *Syndicat d'initiative* in Monflanquin there were more roses. They framed the election posters from which smiled M. Chirac and M. Mitterand and steely-eyed M. Le Pen. Everyone was pleased about the release of the French hostages whose faces and number of days in captivity had been shown after the TV news every night since their capture. We felt sad that the British hostages were not so remembered. It was assumed that M. Mitterand would win the presidency but there was an air of real excitement.

Sunday was the day of the election and we were invited down to the farm to watch the results which, we were surprised to learn, would be declared that evening. Raymond, who obviously had complete faith in the system, explained that it was possible to estimate the results. Thinking of our own all night vigils and last minute demands for recounts I could not understand it.

When we arrived just before eight that evening the table was laid but they had clearly not yet eaten. On the stove was a pot of soup which Claudette, intent on the screen, made no attempt to heat or serve. Raymond turned to greet us. '*Asseyez-vous, asseyez-vous,*' he said hastily, pulling out more chairs. Grandma, hands folded in her lap, her head on one side like a little patient bird, sat leaning towards the screen with its fast-talking commentator. Grandpa, putting down the cat he was stroking, got up to turn up the volume.

Moments later a thinly smiling M. Chirac elegantly and sonorously conceded defeat, making it seem, in the manner of politicians everywhere, that it was almost a triumph. Grandpa laughed. 'What did I tell you?' he crowed.

Not from a presidential desk but jostled by an ecstatic crowd, some jumping up to be seen on camera, calm paternal M. Mitterand spoke to the nation. After that it was a free-for-all. In the next hour of chauvinism, mere party politics irrelevant, it was *la gloire de la France*, past, present and future that was extolled. We imagined the eighty-five per cent of the population that had voted listening as *les*

Bertrand listened with shining eyes. Grandpa did something that I had never seen him do before. Without a word he got up from his chair, lit the gas under the soup, stirred the pot and then served himself, watching the television all the while.

'Well I always thought that food was the most important thing in France,' said Mike. 'Now I know it's politics.'

Raymond laughed, *'Bien sûr, mais ce n'est pas tous les jours.'*

At last the transmission ended. Claudette came out of her trance and in her usual brisk fashion she prepared a meal. As on most Sunday evenings, except for special occasions, it consisted chiefly of leftovers from lunch. My contribution, a chocolate cake, tempted Véronique, my one-time rosy-cheeked little *professeur de dictée*, now quite a beauty, who came in briefly for yet another change of clothes. Raymond opened a bottle of his sweet golden wine, *fabrication maison* from Anaïs's grapes, to drink with the cake and talked about his plans to sow *le grand champ* with sunflowers. 'And what about the newly cleared ground just below the wood?'

'Sunflowers too,' he said, 'but they'll have to be planted later as the soil is heavier and still too wet.' Clearly sunflowers were profitable as well as spectacular. 'You'll be surrounded by sunflowers,' he said, 'that will please you.'

As we said goodnight and came out to the car a nightingale was singing. We freewheeled down the drive and sat leaning out and listening to the miraculous sound, reluctant to start the engine and shatter the night with mechanical noise.

A few days later, hired by the farmers' *Coopérative*, another new machine and its driver arrived. With its gleaming red containers it sowed eight rows at a time, blowing each seed through a revolving perforated disc which ensured its falling to earth at exactly spaced intervals. As the young man drove down the field, Raymond, hands on hips, very much the successful *patron*, watched contentedly, the first eight rows of sunflowers already in his mind's eye. But when the machine turned and the long straight lines began to waver his face changed. He threw his hands in the air, '*Oh, comme il est maladroit!*' he cried, clearly wishing he was doing the job himself. He turned his back on the field and came in for an aperitif. 'Now we need rain,' he said, 'then in eight days they will have germinated.' The next thing, as though to order, I heard the first heavy drops pattering onto my terrace as I fell asleep. The seeds sown by high technology germinated as predicted, but on the tenth day I was amused to see Raymond, a basket on his arm like some biblical sower, trudging the perimeter of *le grand champ* scattering slug-killer.

We bought twenty square metres of small, square brick tiles to cover the floor of the new *atelier* and the west facing porch, and Le Barbu being otherwise occupied, Mike became M. René's new assistant. Their only problem was the low beam which formed the outer edge of the porch roof. With the floor level raised it was now almost lethal, and in spite of constant cries of *attention* everyone cracked their head.

'We'll have a go at raising it in the summer,' said M. René as he grouted the tiles with liquid cement, forcing it into the cracks with a large squeegee. Then it was all hands to cleaning them, first with sawdust, then on our knees with rags soaked in fuel oil. Rough fired and marked with the odd cinder, the tiles are simple and attractive and we were pleased with the result of our working holiday.

Before our return that summer I went to Granada in June to work on a television film and I spent my one free day walking round the magnificent gardens of the Alhambra in a disbelieving trance. Later on our journey down to Bel-Air in July we called at Giverny and once again I was stunned by another ravishing garden, the one which Claude Monet designed. Yet for me neither of these compared with the experience of climbing our winding track overhung with sunflowers. I think that no one could walk the length of such a field without a lifting of the spirits. The vigour of the tough stems draped with large broadly-veined leaves, the bee-studded centres brown at the outside edge where they begin to ripen, shading inwards to palest green, the exuberant luxury of the overlapping petals with the late afternoon sun behind them, the hot ripe scent of marigolds – all must be enjoyed the more intensely for in a few weeks they will be dry dark mockery of their former perfection. There is a primitive joy about a flower whose head is as large as one's own. *Les tournesols?* They do not turn. They lift their faces to the morning sun and stay there and are glorious. And we were doubly lucky for as those in *le grand champ* began to fade, those planted later on the other side of the house opened. It was a golden summer.

A week after we arrived Grandpa celebrated his eightieth birthday. Twenty-nine adults and seven children sat trying to decipher the menu. Véronique, after specially naming each dish – *foie gras entier de canard* became *délices de Barbarie*, intelligible presumably to those familiar with this species of duck, the salmon was *seigneur de la rivière* – had then written the titles backwards. The guests puzzled over the long list of dishes. One held it up to a mirror. 'It's in English,' shouted another.

'It's not,' we cried. The wife of *le garagiste* shrugged and smiled.

'I shan't bother,' she said, 'I know it will all be delicious. I shall just sit here and eat it.' So did we all, course after course after course, and wine after wine, a 1960 Burgundy, tawny and wonderful and a Chateau Margaux '78 with *le rôti*. Eighty years called for such a celebration.

Le garagiste, now retired, has taken to travelling and regaled us with tales of tropical fish seen from glass-bottomed boats in Guadeloupe. His brother, a retired peripatetic *inséminateur*, now stays put and studies bees. He will talk about his hives and his honey with mounting enthusiasm for as long as you will listen. A dragonfly lighted briefly on the table and he was off, describing its lifecycle as though it were one of the wonders of the world, which it is.

Inevitably they talked of wine, and the problems of those growers who were introducing hybrids to improve the quality. But what, in fact was happening to that quality? They threw their hands in the air. 'Bordeaux? A disgrace!' said someone. They looked at each other.

'Of course,' said the bee-keeper, local pride reasserting itself, *'un bon Bordeaux* is always superior to *un Bourgogne.'* They nodded. *'Mais un bon, j'ai dit,'* he roared, finger poised, 'with nine out of ten Bourgognes *on est sûr, la même avec le Cognac, mais le Bordeaux — attention!'* No one moved, shocked by such perfidy, but there was worse. *'Armagnac aussi,'* he shouted. They shook their heads in despair. *'Maintenant,'* he finished solemnly, *'il faut toujours savoir le terroir et le cru.'*

The champagne was poured as they nodded agreement. The bee-keeper, clearly the family orator, took a much altered script from his pocket, put on a pair of glasses which looked far too small on his broad, mobile face and began his peroration to Grandpa with the somewhat inaccurate statement, 'We have known you now for eighty years — we marvel at your youth.' Grandpa laughed and looked at his plate.

All summer visitors came and went as the sunflowers ripened, the seed-heads swelling and darkening, plums began to scent the air and the maize dried and crackled in the heat; family and friends, actors and architects, poets, painters, psychologists and priests and, *en passant,* friends of friends, curious about this place that they had heard of called Bel-Air. Claudette delighted in sampling each new dish that we prepared for her. She was fascinated by steak and kidney pie and a Portugese recipe for potted sardines in whole lemons and also my cousin David's avocados mixed with sharp apple, watercress and toasted nuts. Raymond demanded more mince pies. Their interest in food is insatiable. On their return from a visit to friends their account of the day will inevitably begin with *'On a très bien mangé,'* and will continue with many a *'et puis, et puis.'* I am sure that they would never think of eating, as Mike and I do when we are busy, a tin of tuna emptied onto a bowl of green salad, a squeeze of lemon and a sliced onion. We eat, enjoy and go back to work. This is not *le système d'ici!*

The sunflowers burned almost black and were harvested leaving a field of stalks which Raymond chopped all day in a swirl of dust. The following day, while he began the plum harvest, we decided to begin working on the west terrace with M. René. The more we looked at the state of the timbers of the porch roof the more sensible it seemed to replace them when we raised the dangerous beam. Clearly when *le charpentier* had originally done the whole roof twelve years previously he had either run out of enthusiasm or money by the time he had reached that end of the building. Now that the old prune oven was to be used as a studio it was essential to make it watertight and dustproof. We looked up at the smoke-blackened triangle of crumbling rough-cast at the very top of the wall. That too would look so much better if we cleaned it off. Now we realised that we should have done all this work before tiling the floor.

We bought £80 worth of new roof timbers, *chevrons et voliges*, rafters and laths. We laid a plastic sheet over our brick-tiled floor and then covered it with the new wood. The demolition began. I soon realised just how heavy Roman terracotta roof tiles are, as I helped to remove and stack them. The old worm-eaten roof timbers made another stack of firewood and then we jacked up the heavy beam until the tallest of us could pass beneath it. As we began to tap away the dirty rough-cast the handsome stones beneath emerged. As we worked down the wall we uncovered the hand-cut stones of an early archway. We repointed the stones with a cream cement and them M. René and Le Barbu rebuilt the roof.

They started before eight-thirty in the morning, worked until midday when M. René drank an aperitif, and then disappeared. They began again at two and worked until eight. When I brought them lemon tea and biscuits at five they accused me of teaching them bad habits, but they drank the tea. There was a slight problem next day when they replaced the tiles. For some obscure reason they each began at opposite ends. This did not matter with the underneath, stop tiles, for they lock into place, but the curved canal tiles can be overlapped as little or as much as one wishes. It was Mike who realised that there would be a problem when they met, or rather did not meet, in the middle. I went for a walk while he pointed this out as tactfully as possible and we helped them begin again. '*Impeccable!*' said M. René happily when it was finished. And it was.

My sister and her husband arrived for a week with enough clothes for a month, not sure what weather to expect at the very end of September. The plum machine shook the last tree, folded its wings and hibernated. The last few plums which fell to earth stayed there as Raymond busied himself with greasing the *montecharge*, the elevator, and dragging it out of the barn. He cleared the ground around the base of *le crib*, the tall, narrow cage in which the corn cobs are stored, the grain being stripped later. The harvester and driver arrived the following morning, and the elevator was positioned so that the cobs would drop into the end of the crib. I went down to the edge of the field of maize to watch the first cut.

   High in his cabin the driver grinned and waved. The wide machine, scarlet against the blue sky, had four glistening steel rockets on the front. The driver lowered his sights and charged. Four rows of stalks ten feet tall went down like feathers and the cobs were stripped. When the machine was full the back rose up to disgorge the golden shower into a waiting trailer which in its turn carried the load and tipped it into the base of the elevator. The cobs flowed upwards to tumble at the top into the cage. Raymond was everywhere, the first section almost full he ran up the ladder to rake the piled cobs flat and lower the first roof section to protect them, then down again to attend to the machine which had stopped. Something was jammed. He threw the motor into reverse and restarted it. 'Could someone pick up those?' he pleaded, pointing to the cobs which had missed the crib. Someone could. It made a change from lifting roof tiles.

The first section full, the elevator was repositioned and all the loose grain underneath had to be shovelled into a sack. Someone else, my brother-in-law, volunteered. 'What a pity you don't have any chicken,' shouted Raymond as he hauled the elevator into place and switched it on to propel another yellow stream upward. Tractors and trailers trundled to and fro. Everything was motion until without warning the elevator stopped again. Now it seemed it would only work in reverse. What to do? My sister and I, not in the least bit interested in machines that don't work, sat chatting, while the men, including the combine driver, held conference. Various remedies were suggested but in the end they reversed all the wiring and once again the corn cobs clattered to the top where Raymond leapt about with his rake.

With only one more trailer full to unload, the field a massacre of broken and twisted stalks and empty paper sheaths, the elevator once again hiccupped and was silent. Raymond cursed. It was almost dark. The only possible solution was to couple it to the drive of the tractor, itself twenty years old. As the final load inched its way up we heaved a sigh of relief. The last strip of sunset faded and we shivered in a sudden breeze which had a touch of autumn.

Supper for fifteen was ready at the long table, soup, saucisson, croque monsieur, roast guinea fowl, pommes dauphine and floating island, and we drank our '81 which we had matured in the famous oak barrel for four years. Inevitably Raymond told tales of the corn harvests *d'autrefois* and the communal stripping of the sheaths from the cobs. 'We would all gather in the barn,' he said, 'a great crowd of us. We always ate sardines and bread and what *les jeunes* enjoyed was finding the mouldy cobs, there were always a few, and we would daub our faces with them.' He sighed.

Even as the farmers in this region of *la polyculture* group together to buy sophisticated machinery, as they enlarge and modernise their *coopératives* for processing their grapes and plums, as they change crops to take advantage of financial inducements, soya beans, strawberries and sunflowers replacing wheat and tobacco, their pride in the new is tempered by a real nostalgia. At local midsummer *fêtes* the old and not so old delight in demonstrations of ancient machinery. Dressed in their best clothes they reminisce, seeming to enjoy being covered in chaff and dust as sweating volunteers hurl forks full of wheat into a snorting clanking steam-driven threshing machine. The very old laugh. To them even this is modern. They can remember machines pulled by oxen, a child following behind with an old saucepan to catch the excrement lest it spoil the wheat, and the great meals that were served afterwards for twenty or thirty harvesters, and always the best wines from *la cave*. '*Ah les beaux jours d'autrefois,*' they sigh as they go home in their Volvos and Renaults and telephone the entrepreneur to see when the combine harvester might arrive.

Only *la vendange* still has something of the olden days about it, as we had discovered. The last grapes were to be picked on Monday and we would leave on the following day. All day Sunday while we closed the other bedrooms, covering the beds with plastic sheets and putting the linen and pillows in lavender scented chests, Claudette was cooking. She and Grandma even made two *tourtières*. It was not only the last day of *la vendange* but the last harvest meal of the year. 'And we shall be able to relax,' said Raymond, 'the grapes are for *vin de Pays, les Cabernets Sauvignon et les Merlots*. We don't have very many and we shall be finished by midday. That will please Mme Barrou,' he laughed.

Next morning as we were waiting to start we were introduced to a farmer whose land adjoins our own. I recognised him but I had never seen his wife, a sad creature with gnarled hands and cruelly veined legs. She was very shy and her French was difficult to understand. Eventually she told me that she was, like her husband, originally from Italy. He had been brought by his parents as a baby but she, without a word of French, had come when she was eighteen to be married. 'I was so lonely,' she said.

'Do you remember Anaïs at Bel-Air?' I asked.

'Of course,' she smiled, 'she would wave to me but I could not speak to her. I could not make friends.'

Mme Barrou roared into the courtyard on her Solex as the bee-keeper, *le garagiste* and their wives arrived in an ex-Post Office van. Carrying our baskets we walked down to the vineyard and began. 'I am getting past this,' said the bee-keeper, puffing slightly. 'I only come to pick these because they were planted on *les hautes tiges*, not so much bending!'

'I love *la vendange*,' said his wife, 'you know that once it is in everything is done, and it's not too hot to work.' The air was soft and warm, the pickers as mature as the grapes and we worked at a leisurely pace. The bell for midday sounded from the church and Mme Barrou decided to go home to change her working dress before lunch. Walking back to the house I found it hard to believe that in two days I would be back in London. We had been here for three months, our longest stay ever.

There were wonderful smells in the dining room. Everyone smiled in anticipation. As he passed me an aperitif Raymond whispered, 'you will sing, Ruth, won't you? It's the last day. I'm warning you beforehand so you can think about it.' He smiled half-apologetic, half-mischievous. It ruined my appetite but not for long. I knew the acoustics were good. If I were singing on some after-dinner engagement in London I would be outside waiting while everyone else ate, worrying about the state of the piano, the band and the microphone. Here there were none of these.

Unaccompanied I sang the songs which over the years I have learned that they love, *'J'attendrai'*, *'Le Temps des Cerises'* and *'Le Blé d'Or'*. I was sitting opposite my Italian neighbour and when for her I sang *'Santa Lucia'* her eyes filled with tears. Claudette, passing behind me with the coffee pot hissed, *'Chantez "Granada"*, Ruth.' Heaven help me! We had listened to 'Granada' sung with an expert

flamboyance by José Carreras on television a few nights
before. But how could I refuse? I would never have an
audience like this in London. These are not well-to-do
sophisticates out for an evening's diversion. I look at their
faces, their hands. Our backs ache and we have worked
together, and they are kind people. I sing and am grateful
for such an audience.

That night, as though they know we are leaving, there
is a mouse in the bathroom and a tree-frog on the bedroom
shutter. What will we enjoy in London? Our other home.
Other friends and neighbours, a piano, the theatre, concerts
and everything else that London offers. Carpets, central
heating, good television and work, if there is any, will ease
us through the first cold months of the new year.

As the days warm and lengthen we shall begin to think
about returning to Bel-Air. We know that whatever happens
in the coming year it will be there, tucked into the hillside,
its head down against the westerlies, waiting to restore us
all. The cats and owls will chase the mice in the attics which
we leave open for the clean sweet air to blow through. *Les
Bertrand* will telephone, '*il fait beau, le coucou est arrivé, vous
venez?*' And we shall begin making plans.

A la prochaine fois!

Appendix
Useful Information

The author cannot claim to be an expert on buying property in France but the following information may be useful.

Looking for a property
In France estate agents' charges are much higher than in England. Controls have been abolished and commission may vary between 4% and 10%. Even higher charges are not unheard of. Usually the cheaper the property the higher the percentage. Detailed descriptions of properties are not often provided but agents are prepared to drive prospective clients around all day in the hope of a sale. Bargains can still be found but only in relatively undiscovered areas. With good French it might also be possible to buy direct from the vendor, but beware of the farmer whose long empty property awaits *un pigeon*, someone with more money than sense. There are a number of expatriate English entrepreneurs who know what is available in their own area, and the list of estate agents in England dealing in French property grows longer every week.

Deciding on a property
The choice of house is, of course, an entirely personal affair. If in any doubt don't buy, might be good advice. Article 1642 of the *Code Civil* protects a vendor against all liability for obvious defects so it is important for the buyer to check for these and bargain accordingly. There are no professional surveyors in France. If in any doubt an architect or a builder should be consulted. Hidden defects which the buyer could be expected not to notice at once are however the

responsibility of the vendor. There is a ten year guarantee for structural faults and a two year guarantee for internal fixtures on new buildings. Attractive but isolated cottages and barns may not have water, electricity or sanitation.

Water
In France, water is metered, therefore a working well can be more than just a decorative feature. To be connected to a nearby mains the regional office of SOGEA must be contacted. A simple *branchement d'eau*, bringing water to the outside of the property, will cost approximately 5000 francs.

Electricity
There is a charge of 3800 francs for a connection to the property. To bring electricity any distance the cost is 8000 francs for each pole, normally distanced at 200/250 metres, and 50 francs for each metre of cable. If the property is more than 60 metres from the nearest supply some small communes, keen to attract more residents, will pay up to 50% of the cost of installation. For this they must be affiliated to the *Syndicat d'Électricité Rurale*. The local Mayor is the person to consult on this and every other matter of French bureaucracy.

Sanitation
If the property is on the edge of a small town it may be possible to be connected to the mains sewage system. In some towns this is free, in others the full cost must be paid. It depends on the decision of the local council. More usually it will be necessary to have a septic tank, *une fosse septique*, installed by the local builder, or *maçon*, which will then be connected to the house by the *plombier*.'

Buying the property
Once the decision is made an agreement, *le compromis de vente*, must be signed by both parties and a deposit of 10% paid. Once signed both parties are committed. If the vendor pulls out he must return the deposit. If the buyer pulls out

he loses his deposit. Before signing it is advisable to check all the clauses with the solicitor, *le notaire*. A list of *notaires* in each region an be obtained from the *Chambre Interdédepartmentales des Notaires de Paris* [telephone Paris 231 88 02], 12 Avenue Victoria, Paris 75007.

For the final conveyancing the *notaire* will act for both parties, which speeds up the process, but his fees are for the buyer to pay. They include a government tax on land, and according to the value of this will vary between 8% and 14% of the purchase price.

Restoration

For any property already classified as a ruin or for any substantial additions to an existing property a *permis de construire* is required. The mayor will advise. Before making drastic alterations, consideration of climate and prevailing winds may be wise. Most very old houses were built the way they are for good reasons. In the south particularly it may be prudent to wait until it is 90° in the shade before deciding to enlarge the windows. At least one cool dark room may be essential.

Le charpentier will fix the roof.

Le menuisier will make shutters and doors.

Le carreleur will tile the floors. But with all of them an estimate, *un devis*, is advisable.

Rates and taxes

Local rates vary from region to region. *Les Impôts Locaux* are divided into two parts:

1 *Le Tax d'Habitation* which is based on the size of the property and its amenities: bathroom, garage, pool etc. A large portion of this tax goes to benefit the local commune.
2 *Les Taxes Foncières* which is a land tax providing funds for a larger region. As it says on the bill: for *la commune, le département, la région et divers organismes*!

If the property is isolated the track leading up to it may be part of *le chemin rurale de la commune*. If so the owner is entitled to a free load of stones every two years. The mayor must write the necessary order to the nearest quarry. He will also provide a *permis de résidence* which is useful when bringing small items of furniture through customs. Secondhand furniture is often very expensive in France.

Finally, if you have no French I would urge you to learn. Imagine how much a French family buying a cottage in rural England would miss if they did not understand a word of the language. I suggest hat no matter how much the new residents smiled, even the friendliest of locals would eventually tire of being addressed in French, however loudly or slowly. And if, like me, becoming really fluent looks like taking you the rest of your life, what more stimulating way to spend it.

Bonne aventure!